CONVERSATIONS WITH MY SONS AND DAUGHTERS

MAMPHELA RAMPHELE

PENGUIN BOOKS

PENGUIN BOOKS

Published by the Penguin Group
Penguin Books (South Africa) (Pty) Ltd, Block D, Rosebank Office Park, 181 Jan Smuts Avenue,
Parktown North Johannesburg 2193, South Africa
Penguin Group (USA) Inc, 375 Hudson Street, New York, New York 10014, USA
Penguin Group (Canada), 90 Eglinton Avenue East, Suite 700, Toronto, Ontario, Canada M4P 2Y3 (a
division of Pearson Penguin Canada Inc)
Penguin Books Ltd, 80 Strand, London WC2R 0RL, England
Penguin Ireland, 25 St Stephen's Green, Dublin 2, Ireland (a division of Penguin Books Ltd)
Penguin Group (Australia), 2707 Collins Street, Melbourne, Victoria 3008, Australia (a division of
Pearson Australia Group Pty Ltd)
Penguin Books India Pvt Ltd, 11 Community Centre, Panchsheel Park, New Delhi – 110 017, India
Penguin Group (NZ), 67 Apollo Drive, Rosedale, Auckland 0632, New Zealand (a division of Pearson
New Zealand Ltd)

Penguin Books (South Africa) (Pty) Ltd, Registered Offices:
Block D, Rosebank Office Park, 181 Jan Smuts Avenue, Parktown North Johannesburg 2193, South Africa

www.penguinbooks.co.za

First published by Penguin Books (South Africa) (Pty) Ltd 2012
Reprinted 2012 (five times), 2013 (twice)

Copyright © Mamphela Ramphele 2012

ISBN 978-0-14-353041-1

Cover by mrdesign
Cover photograph by Morne van Zyl
Printed and bound by UltraLitho, Johannesburg

CONTENTS

INTRODUCTION

Mabu a u tswitswe! These words haunted me for a good week or so. They were uttered early in 2011 by a young professional man with a pensive look on his face. He felt no need to explain the context of these weighty words. He assumed that I would understand his distress and its source. This Sepedi idiom – which literally means 'the soil has been stolen' – is used as a call to action to defend the land following the assassination of a king by a conquering power. All able-bodied men would be expected to prepare to avenge the outrage and reclaim the land from the usurpers.

Why would this idiom be used by a young South African in 2011?

I believe he was reflecting the sentiments of many young South African professionals and business people as well as a significant proportion of those in the public sector. An air of despair is settling into the society that has been the pride of many freedom lovers across the globe since its transition to democracy in 1994. The excitement of watching a country that had been written off as hopelessly trapped in an unwinnable conflict between the white minority apartheid regime and the largely black majority rise against all odds to take bold steps towards becoming a constitutional democracy, is giving way to anxiety. Not even memories of the inspirational leadership of the iconic Nelson Mandela can hide the growing sense of disappointment that the dream of freedom has yet to be reflected in the everyday lives of the majority of the population. After more than a decade and a half of transition to democracy cracks are showing in the system of governance that threaten the idealism on which the society reinvented itself.

Governance is understood as the exercise of authority with three basic dimensions: political, economic and institutional. The *political dimension* is measured through indicators for democratic accountability, political stability and absence of major conflict and violence in society. The *economic dimension* reflects government effectiveness and the quality of the regulatory framework and its execution. The *institutional dimension* refers to matters pertaining to the rule of law, the control of corruption and the strengths of public institutions that underpin good order. Worldwide research has shown that good governance is associated with a significant development dividend, especially in the medium to long term. Over the last decade or so South Africa has been showing signs of decline in its performance as a well-governed country. State capture in the political, economic and institutional dimensions is becoming a reality of our society.

One need look no further than the government's own National Planning Commission's Diagnostic Report released in June 2011 which lists a number of issues that signal the trend towards the kind of decline that brought down the Hapsburg Empire in Europe and the post-colonial state in Latin America and Africa. Indicators to watch are:

- Rising corruption
- Weakening of state and civil society institutions
- Poor economic management
- Skills and capital flight
- Politics dominated by short-termism, ethnicity or factionalism
- Lack of maintenance of infrastructure and standards of service

The most disquieting overall finding by the National Planning Commission is that poverty and inequality persist. This means that despite a commitment to promote progressive realisation of socio-economic rights as set out in our national constitution, the majority of South Africans remain poor and marginalised. Social justice remains elusive eighteen years after the attainment of freedom. Why? The most important reasons identified by all political parties in the run-up to the 2009 national elections, as well as by the Dinokeng Scenarios sponsored by Old Mutual and Nedbank in 2009, are:

- The quality of education for poor South Africans leaves much to be desired. A key reason for this is dysfunction in 80 per cent of schools with teachers often not in class, not well prepared to teach, and not competent to use the relevant teaching aids.
- Too few South Africans have employment, especially amongst the youth where for 15 to 24 years old the unemployment rate was 51.3 per cent in 2010 and 29 per cent for the 25 to 34-year-olds.

The result is that more than three million young people between the ages of 15 and 35 years are not in education, not in employment and not in training.

- Poorly located and inadequate infrastructure perpetuates apartheid's racially engineered geographic divisions and limits social inclusion and the rate of economic growth.
- High levels of crime and insecurity, especially amongst poor people who remain excluded from the benefits of basic public services.

The underperformance of the post-apartheid government in the social sectors and infrastructure for poor communities lies at the heart of persistent poverty and growing inequality. The excellent job the government has done in stabilising the macro-economic framework, establishing disciplined fiscal management and developing policies to underpin economic development has enhanced the performance of the economy as measured by GDP growth as a middle-income country. The benefits of this growth have gone disproportionately to middle and upper-class citizens. The losers are unskilled entrants into the economy who face high barriers of entry and are the first to lose out when recessions hit.

Growing inequality undermines the foundations of social justice and stability in the country. The South African Institute of Race Relations (SAIRR) Survey for 2009/2010 shows that annual per capita income rose for all racial categories between 1996 and 2009 with changes of 270 per cent for Africans and 229 per cent for white people. The growing inequality stems from the low income base of R5 847 for Africans growing to R21 516 versus the R43 052 base for white people growing to R141 592.[1] The legacy of inequality simply breeds more inequality even as the economy and personal incomes grow. It will take a fundamental transformation of socio-economic relations to reduce these levels of inequality.

The young man's cryptic statement that 'the soil has been stolen' is informed by these grim statistics and general despair about the government's lack of visible political will to address the issues. But why did this young man express himself in this idiom? Are we really facing a major national crisis? Why did he direct his anguish to me? I can only assume that he believed that I share his understanding of the state of our nation, and perhaps hoped that I could initiate an intergenerational conversation about where we are as a people. In some ways, this idiom best captures his understanding that in a constitutional democracy the citizens are the sovereigns. It is their sovereignty that is at stake and they need to be called to action to defend their democracy.

Let us describe this young man in greater detail because he represents many others who keep the same question hidden in their anxious minds. We shall call him Matome. He is in his late thirties and lives in Johannesburg's suburb of Melville with his young wife. They have postponed having children in order to consolidate their relationship and professions first. Matome has worked hard to qualify as a financial analyst with one of the major companies in the country. He is a committed patriot who has been watching the slide of our society into poor governance, growing social ills such as crime and insecurity, and unemployment especially among young people, including those with higher education qualifications. The bright future he saw so clearly ten years ago is becoming dimmer and dimmer.

Matome is finding little comfort from his peers who advise him to keep his head down, focus on his career, and not jeopardise his great prospects of reaching the very top. He is reminded that becoming involved in civic matters would annoy the many clients that his company has attracted over the years. He is reminded of the examples of career limitations that befell other young professionals within both the private and public sectors who had dared to challenge practices that benefited big people. He is torn between his conscience that would like him to speak up and his personal and professional interests that may be put at risk by such an action.

We spend two hours talking through his dilemma to enable him to articulate his concerns and weigh up his options. He is under no illusion that his generation will have to engage with all the issues confronting the country he loves so much. He knows that he is not alone in being caught in this dilemma, but is also acutely aware that fear of the unknown is preventing his generation from stepping up to the plate and being heard. He nonetheless commits to raising the alarm and drawing strength in numbers as more and more of his peers begin to listen with greater interest and show signs of readiness to commit to at least exploring what young citizens of their generation could do to stop the slide into a failed democracy.

He lays the root cause of the declining performance in governance in our society at the door of the assassins of the citizen as sovereign. Who are these assassins? They are those who have captured the state. Capture of the polity is characterised by a patronage-driven system in which a small ruling elite, political associates, legislators and public servants are provided with jobs in return for loyalty, regardless of their performance. Capture of key sectors of the economy follows from the extension of these clientelistic practices into the private sector domain, including state-owned enterprises, for the benefit of a minority at the expense of the majority. In the apartheid era the white minority benefited. Today, many of them continue to benefit but major new entrants are those who are politically well-connected – both black and white.

Two examples show the extent to which state capture has become embedded in South Africa's governance system. Let us look at Julius Malema of the African National Congress Youth League (ANCYL), who is becoming larger than life both physically and politically. He has been handsomely rewarded for the major role he played in campaigning for Jacob Zuma to become president of the African National Congress (ANC) in 2008 and, a year later, president of the country despite over-whelming evidence that he had a case to answer with respect to his business/political dealings with convicted fraudster, Shabir Shaik:

> Julius Malema, the President of the ANC Youth League, a native of Limpopo, was exposed by the *City Press* in mid-2011 as having captured the province's polity and economy. He literally installed his friend, Cassel Mathale, as Premier after the 2009 elections as a conduit to taking control of the Limpopo Province's Department of Roads and Transport budget totalling R11.6bn and that of the Department of Health at a modest R3.6bn. He was given a R50m contract through his company On-Point Engineering to operate a Program Management Unit (PMU). On-Point Engineering is run by his friend Lesiba Cuthbert Gwagwa with a mandate to allocate tenders for jobs ranging from road maintenance to health infrastructure.[2] In addition to the fee paid by the Limpopo Province to On-Point Engineering, each recipient of a tender enters into an agreement with it to pay 50-90% of any profit made on the tenders into Ratanang Trust, which is controlled by Julius Malema. Ratanang is the name of Malema's young son.
>
> Julius Malema has established himself as the most successful young tenderpreneur. He scored more than R140m from 21 tenders in 31

municipalities in Limpopo Province in the 2008/2009 fiscal year under the umbrella of SGL, a company he ran with the same friend. They tendered for a variety of projects including building a fire station, bridges, street paving, with neither engineering nor construction skills between them. Many of the projects they were involved in were found to be in a shocking state, including bridges that have been washed away and collapsed structures. SGL has not been held to account for any of these failed projects.

Malema flaunts his wealth in the most disturbing way. He lives in an expensive suburb, Sandown, and has just demolished a house he bought a year or so ago for millions to build one reputed to cost close to R16m. He drives expensive cars, wears expensive labels and drinks only the most pricy liquor. He refuses to account to anyone and simply says he does not care about who says what.

When asked how this impunity is possible, senior ANC member and former cabinet minister Sydney Mufumadi could only say that 'It is a phenomenon that has become widespread across the country. Those who don't have the skills or entrepreneurship to produce are buying access to politicians so that they can access the tendering system that way. And our society is not only becoming one that consumes, but we are now in the early stages of a dangerous kleptocracy.'[3] A culture of impunity is taking root at every level in government. It is this kleptocracy that is at the heart of the 'stolen soil' of which the young man Matome, referred to above, was speaking.

Julius Malema has been untouchable since the 2008 ANC National Conference in Polokwane precisely because he is emulating what is common practice in government and the ruling party. The most disturbing example from which he takes his lead is Chancellor House, an ANC front for Black Economic Empowerment (BEE) deals to fund the ruling party.

Chancellor House was formed in 2003 under Thabo Mbeki's presidency. It takes its name from the building in which Nelson Mandela and his partner Oliver Tambo had their legal practice in the 1950s. The key players in Chancellor House are trusted loyalists of the Mbeki era ANC who posed as legitimate business people. Investments listed on the website detailing its history and activities are in mining, in which many new order mineral rights were granted to it, and in logistics and infrastructure areas in which the government is regulator and player. The most visible of the deals is the Eskom R20 billion Medupi Power Station financed by the World Bank in which Chancellor House is a 25 per cent BEE partner. Valli Moosa, then Eskom Chair, is also a key player in Chancellor House. Beyond the obvious conflict of interest of granting Chancellor House such a lucrative deal from a state-owned enterprise, the capture of the state by the ruling party takes on a level of impunity that is frightening.

Members of the post-2009 Zuma ANC, led by Mathews Phosa, the treasurer-general, publicly committed that the ANC would audit and exit the investments to stop the undermining of good governance by having a ruling party use its position to be both player and referee (in the BEE space). No such exit has occurred and state capture continues to undermine the basic tenets of our constitutional democracy. How can opposition parties compete with a ruling party that is using state resources to make it invincible?

In a cynical stance, many government officials, including some in the Department of Trade and Industry, bemoan the abuse of the BEE legislative framework by those who front as legitimate BEE beneficiaries. How can the government get to grips with this problem while the ruling party is 'fronter-in-chief'?[4]

The young man Matome has reason to be depressed and to speak of the assassination of the citizen as the sovereign of our constitutional democracy. Those in power show scant regard for the citizen as a voter to whom they should be accountable – as Malema says, 'I do not care!' The assassins have rendered the citizen irrelevant – as good as dead.

This book of conversations is a response to this young man and many other young women and men who are struggling to understand how their country has come to this from those heady post-1994 Madiba Magic days. They see the dream of a prosperous society united in its diversity in a dynamic democratic order vanishing with the revelation of each new scandal that makes previous ones look minor. Where will it end?

It is my hope that the call to action by this young man will be heeded by his peers. Citizens need to engage in reasoned conversations about what matters and how we, as the sovereigns of this land, can act to stop the risks that are threatening our dreams. We need to shift the frame of reference from the politics of fear and patronage, to assert ourselves as sovereigns and defend our constitutional democracy. We need to signal a shift from subjects to citizens and be ready to undertake the journey to the future we envisage for ourselves.

A good place to start our conversations is to revisit a few key issues:

- The values of our national constitution
- Why are there such large gaps between values and practice?
- How does a society rebirth itself?
- What would a transformational journey – generational, political, socio-economic – look like?

We should then conclude with a number of practical suggestions on how we can put ourselves on a turn-around pathway towards the society of our dreams.

CHAPTER 1

SHIFTING THE GROUND OF REASON

South Africa is a country blessed with infinite possibilities which reflect its geographic position on the ancient continent of Africa. It is heir to hidden treasures, both material and spiritual. Its spectacular beauty, accentuated by diverse landscapes across rugged mountains and hills as well as vast plains and coastlines, is irresistible. The blueness of our skies is so striking that it made its way into our hearts through our national anthem. The praises we sing to our blue skies transcended the wounds of our divided past and have been woven into our hopes of healing ourselves through collective action to build a shared future. South Africa's people, with their diversity of cultures, have the capacity to come back from the brink each time the rest of the world threatens to write them off. Our resilience as a society against the odds is our greatest strength.

We stand at a very special moment as a society eighteen years after gaining our freedom to become the nation of our dreams – a nation that can proudly take its place in the community of nations. The vision of our country is clearly spelt out in our highly celebrated national constitution. The country of our dreams is one that is to be known for its unity in diversity, its prosperity built on equality and equity in line with the human rights precepts at the heart of our constitution.

Our cross-generational engagement through the conversations this book introduces is aimed at reminding you, the generation who will be the leaders in the twenty-first century, of your rich heritage and to urge you to take ownership of shaping the future of our great country.

There is urgency in these conversations. First, South Africa's infinite possibilities can only become realities if each and every citizen plays the role that citizenship demands from us. The idea that we can out-source our democratic responsibilities to a government or a political party, however committed that government or party might be to the shared dream, is reckless. The dark clouds gathering on our horizons are a reminder that we need to redouble our efforts to make our democracy a success.

Second, I need to remind you, in the words of Frantz Fanon in *The Wretched of the Earth*, that 'Each generation must out of relative obscurity discover its mission, fulfil it, or betray it'.[5] My generation found inspiration in Frantz Fanon in the 1970s and changed the terms of engagement with the struggle for freedom. We redefined the struggle and refocused it on the idea that liberation has to start with the journey to free ourselves from being defined by others and move towards self-definition. We rejected being labelled 'non-whites' or 'non-Europeans' in the country of our birth and rejected the insinuation that being 'white' or 'European' was the standard that we had failed to meet.

We recognised that the first act of freedom was to name ourselves and this process enabled us to describe our own reality. We rejected being constrained by racist notions of what it meant to be black in a world dominated by white power structures. Ours was a generation that had to find its way on a road not well travelled before. We declared that we were black and proud. As Wally Mongane Serote said of the products of Black Consciousness – 'it breathed oxygen' into the flagging anti-apartheid struggle and hastened the dawn of the freedom we enjoy today. It is up to your generation – those of you who are now somewhere between 16 and 40 years old – to define what the focus of your mission is and how you are to fulfil it.

There is no doubt in my mind that a significant proportion of you are searching for definitions of your generation's mission. Conversations with many of you have confirmed my confidence in your determination to do so. You have a very strong platform from which to build the contours of your mission as a generation to whom so much has been bequeathed and of whom so much more is expected. Unlike my generation, many of you have been blessed with more sophisticated higher education, training and role models as well as coaches to help prepare you for your roles.

A key feature of our society today is that the whole is less than the sum of the parts. Our young democracy has achieved much that should make us proud to be its citizens, but realising our full potential requires tough, open conversations about our performance over the last eighteen years since our amazing birth as a new South Africa. We need to be honest about what we have done well and why. Equally, we need to confront what we have not done well, reject excuses for our failures and face up to the reasons for failed policies, failed implementation and failed accountability. It is only through such an honest process of learning the lessons of the past eighteen years that we can map a way forward to become the country of our dreams.

In *Fanonian Practices in South Africa*,[6] Nigel Gibson captured the essence of my inspiration for these cross-generational conversations:

> Just as ongoing struggles over the production of the past include the recovery of radical democratic ideas, cultural forms and experiments in the people's struggle for a new way of life, the struggle over production of the present includes the articulation of new ideas of liberation.

We need to engage in conversations that enable us to go into the treasure trove of our past and recover the ideals that contributed to our greatness. We need equally to see where we lost our idealism and why, and at what cost, that has happened. I will be listening very carefully to your ideas about how we can invigorate the idealism that captured the imagination of so many ordinary men, women and children to give so much to the anti-apartheid struggle in order to secure our future.

What our country needs now is to move away from the politics of convenience towards politics of the principles set out in our founding documents. These principles were largely informed by the dreams of those whose struggles in the streets, on the factory floors, on rural footpaths and across our borders made governing without consent impossible. We need to engage in vigorous 'shifting the ground of reason'[7] to return to the source of our being as freedom-loving people. Ours is a constitutional democracy that embodies the principle of citizens as sovereign and a government by the people for the people.

The critical question is to what extent people are genuinely and meaningfully participating in their own governance. How do you feel about the level of your participation in shaping the future of your country? Is it meaningful and engaged beyond election periods, or are you succumbing to the temptation that seems to have found many takers of being a sleeping shareholder in your country's affairs? Some of you confess to not being engaged citizens for many and varied reasons, at the heart of which is a level of discomfort because politics is 'a dirty game'. Others have a deep sense of fear of the repercussions of open engagement with the critical issues that are impacting on the quality of our democracy. Fear of offending those in government, in the leadership of the governing party, friends and family is widespread in our society.

The irony is that the anti-apartheid struggle was waged by many generations of activists who transcended that fear in the most frightening of circumstances. People exposed themselves to harassment, arrest, torture, and even faced death in order to open the gates to the free society that we enjoy today. My generation of activists broke through the fear that had silenced many after the crushing and banning of historical liberation movements – the ANC, Pan Africanist Congress (PAC) and the South African Communist Party (SACP) as well as the trade union and student formations that had links with them. We openly took on and challenged ourselves to break the chains of 'fear as the determinant of South African politics'.[8] How can we now explain being afraid to exercise the very democratic rights and duties so many fought so hard for? Why are we afraid of our own representatives? Or are we afraid of our own shadows? These are some of the questions that will frame our conversations and help us develop ways forward.

Throughout this book our conversations will be about how we are to re-mobilise citizens to reassert themselves as the sovereigns and share-holders of our country. What role will your generation play in rising to this challenge? What are the tools you can use to make such a reawakening possible and effective in shifting the grounds of reason towards a society you can be proud of? How will we use facts and figures to develop and implement evidence-based policies? How will we ensure honest monitoring and evaluation of our performance without allowing excuses to mask our failures? How will we ensure that there is a strong culture of accountability that will re-establish a link between hard work and excellence in performance to reward?

———————————

These conversations and reflections are an expression of my gratitude to you for giving me the identity of being a mother. In the village of Krantzpoort in Limpopo Province, where I grew up, it was a mark of honour to be known as the 'mother of so and so'. In fact, most indigenous African cultures in South Africa anticipate actual biological motherhood by assigning the name to a newly married woman as (in isiXhosa) *NoPhumzile, NoSiviwe* or (in Sepedi) *MaTlou, MaKarabo*. The reference to adult women as *Bomma* or *Omama* reflects the reverence with which mothers are held in our society.

The sweetness of the first articulation by one's child of the word 'Mama' lingers like an unforgettable melody from the angels and marks the opening of conversations between mothers and their sons or daughters. It is a great asset to African culture that the same sweetness continues to ring from the mouths of young people as a sign of respect for those old enough to be their mothers. Some of my adopted children use the more poetic expression *Motswadi wa ka* – the one who gave birth to me. A better honour for motherhood one cannot imagine – an honour that one should accept with humility.

I am acutely mindful of the pain of those mothers and sisters who have not been blessed with the capacity to bear children. It is a pain that can only be made better by the awareness of the grace that makes acceptance possible. There is comfort from the collective motherhood that is signalled by the loving respectful reference to *Motswadi wa ka* that is inclusive of all women, regardless of whether or not they have their own biological children. There is also the option of adoption, formal or informal, that is open to women today. Adopted children are a priceless gift. I enjoy my adopted children wherever I encounter them – physically or virtually.

I am particularly grateful to two of my daughters for the inspiration to share the reflections in this book. Boni Mehlomakhulu, a former Deputy Director General in the Department of Science and Technology and now CEO of The South African Bureau of Standards (SABS) asked me to mentor her in October 2009 and started a conversation that planted the idea of this book in my mind. I could not agree to mentor her due to time constraints imposed by my many other responsibilities as well as the growing number of similar requests from her peers. She then asked me why I did not write to all my daughters, given the demonstrated hunger for intergenerational role modelling and supportive conversations. The second inspiration for the book came from my daughter, The Light of My Life, Leila Akahloun who, for Christmas 2009, gave me a book, *A Letter to My Daughter* by a Zimbabwean woman, Nozipo Maraire. When I told Leila about Boni's suggestion, she was ecstatic and urged me to make time to write to all my daughters.

After much reflection, I have chosen to write to both my sons and my daughters. I have a growing concern about the social risks attached to not paying attention to both our sons and daughters. Upper and middle-class daughters are beneficiaries of a strong tradition of feminism and the gender equality provisions of our national constitution. Some of our sons are also beneficiaries of the economic benefits of redressing the inequities of the past, but their psycho-social development needs are not adequately attended to. In our society many young men find themselves without any anchors or role models. Many have physically or emotionally absent fathers and grow up in communities where such absence is the norm.

Absent fathers leave a void in young men's lives that mothers often ignore or are unable to address. In fact, 48 per cent of children in South Africa today have living yet absent fathers and only 36 per cent are living with their fathers.[9] According to the 2010/11 Child Gauge, in 2009 only 34 per cent of children were living with both parents.[10] The wound that this absent parent situation inflicts on the majority of children growing up in South Africa needs to be acknowledged and addressed.

The process of social transformation of our society has been weakest in the area of gender relationships. The legacy of traditional male dominance shared by all South Africa's diverse cultures has not been addressed in an appropriate way. Many of the traditions that conflict with the Bill of Rights of our human rights constitutional dispensation have been ignored or fudged. In addition, our society struggles with the radical practical implications of a truly gender equal society as envisaged by our national constitution. Gender equality challenges all citizens to change significant aspects of both their beliefs and behaviours and such a radical change is frightening for most because few of us have had practical experience of living according to the precepts of gender equality. The poisonous mix of race, class and gender in a society with great inequities makes those at the bottom of the social ladder more vulnerable to being victims and perpetrators of gender-based violence. They also fear change more than those who are more secure, which is something we need to acknowledge and engage in conversations about how to transcend it.

This book is also an attempt to redress the tendency to leave sons out of intimate conversations that mothers find easier to have with their daughters. Daughters also feel more comfortable asking their mothers questions about intimate matters than sons tend to do. Traditional attitudes that men cannot share their intimate thoughts and fears with women also put our sons at a disadvantage. Assumptions that sons have fathers to talk to is belied by the reality of increasing numbers of children growing up with absent fathers, as we have mentioned above. The cumulative impact of the migratory labour system and its resultant disruption of family life, weakening of social capital due to poverty and insecurity, and the high levels of divorce and family breakdowns in modern society feed this vicious cycle.

The image of a nuclear two-parent family as the norm is based on analyses informed by studies of predominantly middle-class sectors of the population, but this image is also under strain even in middle-class settings of Western and Northern Hemisphere societies. Sons of single mothers across social classes, of migrant fathers and of emotionally absent fathers are at risk of being short-changed by the focus of mothers on their daughters.

Single mothers, especially African mothers, who loom large (emotionally and figuratively) in desperately poor socio-economic settings, also underestimate the powerful figures they cast within families, communities and societies across the continent. Women's roles as anchors during critical moments, and as reassuring presences in times of uncertainty and fear, leave indelible memories in their children's lives. Many black women have against all odds learnt not only to survive poverty and discrimination, but to do so with an inner core of strength that radiates dignity. It is this powerful image that provides many young girls and women with positive role models, however poor their mothers may be.

What is rarely acknowledged are the complex emotions strong women have evoked in patriarchal societies throughout the ages and across the world. I was reminded of this complexity by the well-written summary of the origins of Candle Mass which was celebrated on 2 February in the Anglican Church's calendar in 2011. This Mass used to be called the Purification Mass marking the day Mary, the Mother of Jesus, brought the child Jesus to the Temple in Jerusalem to be blessed, and for her to be 'purified as was the practice then after the birth of each child'. Jewish culture, like most cultures of the time, reflected the fear of the mythical powers that enabled women to bear children. The Church has been pressured by the feminist movement into changing the name to Candle Mass to focus more on celebrating the Jesus Child as the light of the world, and all children as the gift of light in our lives.

The mythical powers that women are seen to possess have often led to women being labelled as witches, even in post-apartheid South Africa, with tragic consequences. My native province of Limpopo has the notoriety of being the only province in South Africa to have a village dedicated as a place of refuge for women who are at risk of being killed by relatives (including their own sons) and neighbours because they are regarded as witches. Many of these women suffer the fate of being called witches simply for being seen to be too independent, or able to survive as widows or single women without the visible aid of men. This ability to survive in circumstances that few men seem able to cope with is seen as a threat to social order in a male-dominated society. Many of these women are simply surviving on old age pensions and careful management of their few assets. Fear of the power of women is further fuelled by the poor life chances black males experience in a country in which poor education and training outcomes condemn them to a life of poverty and powerlessness.

The reality of the lives of many black men in our patriarchal racist society has left a debilitating legacy for young black men in particular and gender relationships in general. The expectation that they should be the head of the family, its provider and protector is often not met because many poor men lack the capacity and the capability to fulfil these roles. The psycho-social dissonance that is set off in such men and their families by the failure to live up to the dominant male model requires more attention than we have devoted to it. Such men live in a twilight world of pretending to be in charge when they know that they are not, and their families know that too. It is a make-believe world that often breeds resentment and anger against the self and those close to them.

A large proportion of boys and young men in South Africa grow up in homes with such make-believe male heads of households and are thus deprived of the positive role models of strong confident men. The rage and self-hatred generated by displays of weakness by the most significant men in their lives may have serious consequences for young men's present and future relationships with women. Young women from such households cling to the strong mother figure and are often cushioned from the traumas of the lack of a strong father figure. But neither young men nor women are protected from the tendency for abusive social relationships to perpetuate themselves across generations with devastating impacts for society.

Our sons have also become unintended victims of society's programmes to redress the gender inequities that left the girl child behind. For example, 'taking the girl child to work programmes', sensible as they are, begs the question of who takes the boy child to work? This is a particularly critical question given the high levels of unemployment amongst poor people in both urban and rural settings where many young people have not been exposed to working adult role models.

Recent figures from Statistics South Africa indicate that more than three million young people between the ages of 15 and 24 years are not in school, not in training nor at work. Many of these young people come from rural areas or poor urban peripheries where a significant proportion have grown up in homes in which there is no working adult. Young women are over-represented amongst the unemployed youth (63 per cent of 15 to 24-year-old women are unemployed), but we would nonetheless be unwise as a society to ignore the frustrations of young able-bodied men who have aspirations to lead better lives than are currently on offer in a male-dominated society.[11]

The assumption that young black men enjoy the same advantages as the majority of their white counterparts is not borne out by reality. Even middle-class black children have few positive professional role models in their families and communities, given that many are first generation university graduates and professional entrants. Neglecting frustrated and frightened young men undermines the gender equality programme's intentions of broadening the base of participation by young people in the economy. It also heightens the sense of resentment amongst those left out and poses a risk to the stability of our society.

Here, I want to raise an issue beyond the negative motivation of addressing the tragic reality of more than three million young people not being in education programmes, or in training, or employed. This represents wastage of human and intellectual resources that should be applied to enhancing our ability to grow our economy and develop our social and cultural infrastructure to become the prosperous inclusive society we committed ourselves to. Examination of the development trajectories of successful societies points to the critical role of investing in the development of human capabilities as a key success factor. Our post-apartheid government rhetoric of 'people first' (*Batho Pele* in Sesotho) is belied by our failure to address this huge challenge which is also an opportunity for rethinking our development model.

The inclusion of both sons and daughters in the reflections in this book also recognises the need for sons to be nurtured and prepared for partnerships with the type of empowered daughters we are raising. Strong, self-confident young women deserve strong, self-confident young men as peers and partners. Transforming gender relationships requires a fundamental change in the cultural frame of reference that shapes the relationships between men and women and such a process can only be enhanced by deep reflections and conversations between men and women across generations and social classes. Mothers have as much of a vested interest in enabling and supporting their sons as they have in doing so for their daughters. As a single mother of two sons, I am acutely sensitive to the importance of an inclusive approach to raising our children to enable them to face the challenges of our globally connected and rapidly changing world.

These reflections are also inspired by the inadequacy of communication between generations. We have all become too busy to stop, reflect and celebrate our being together in homes, families and communities. Frenetic schedules are not confined to parents, grandparents and other members of the older generations, but extend to our children and grandchildren as well. Their lives are increasingly programmed to include a significant proportion of time outside the family circle and we are all increasingly missing out on the joy of just being together and marvelling at the beauty of togetherness. The 'doing' has overtaken the 'being'. The fireside or kitchen table discussions are too few and far between to enable sustained cross-generational sharing of ideas, insights and experiences.

Our conversations are also about finding a language to speak to matters that frame the relationships between men and women across generations. Gender relationships involve both intimacy and the managing of power dynamics. They are complex relationships because the same person who is the object of love is also a competitor in the power game between men and women. The intensity of the love relationship between a man and a woman sometimes generates an equally intense potential to be a source of hurt and humiliation.

Some feminists make the error of framing gender relationships in terms of power dynamics only. The intimate emotional side of relationships is just as important for it is this that becomes a source of contradiction and compromise that is inexplicable to outsiders. For example, why do so many women stay in abusive relationships for extended periods of time? This goes beyond economic considerations because even women who are economically independent fall into this trap. The secrets of the heart are often not given enough scope in our attempts to understand ourselves and others and, by extension, the complexities of social relationships.

———————————

I have framed these reflections as conversations because they have been informed by real and imagined conversations with many of you as individuals and as groups of individuals – small and large. They reflect the lessons I have learnt from all of you and from generations that have gone before me and I hope they will also form part of our ongoing conversations as you challenge and broaden my understanding through your reactions and responses.

In my reflections I have drawn heavily on African idioms for they are repositories of the wisdom and insights of many generations and are an underutilised treasure trove. I was fortunate to grow up in a family with both sets of grandparents as well as a paternal great-grandmother who shared this wisdom effortlessly through everyday language, proverbs, folklore, bedtime stories and puzzles. My great-grandmother, Tsheola, made the largest contribution to the richness of the heritage that shaped my childhood. She was not only the oldest member of the extended family (she was estimated to be more than a hundred years old when she died), but she delighted in fireside storytelling and in testing our knowledge of riddles and proverbs (*dithai le diema*). All the cultures that make up our diverse nation have much to contribute to our understanding of intergenerational conversations. All we need to do is to claim them, understand them and choose to use what is appropriate to the society we are trying to build together.

We should be extremely concerned as a society about the risk of losing this heritage as part of our multicultural asset base. Too many young parents, especially indigenous Africans, have elected not to teach their children their mother tongues. The convenience of adopting English as the language of choice in the home, school and community comes at the impoverishing cost of growing monolingualism in our society. It is not just the languages that are being lost, but the cultures that go with them and it sends an unfortunate message that progress and upward social mobility should be measured by distance from one's roots. The growing dominance of English as a language of political and economic power is at the heart of the risk we face as a society hurtling towards monolingualism by default.

South Africans seem not to be sufficiently curious about the cultures of fellow citizens. Too few of us make the effort to learn a language outside of what is necessary for our practical needs. Our failing educational system has not helped to encourage young people to explore language diversity at an early stage in life when learning a new language is easier. Many teachers are not fluent in any language, including their own mother tongues and the languages that are the media of instruction. This recycled language incompetence from teachers in many schools serving poor children is detrimental to our social interactions and our ability to engage at a deep level about who we are and what we want to become as a society in transition.

Perhaps we have overdone our confidence-building process of imagining ourselves as a miracle people. Miracles can become sustainable realities through hard work that lives the idealism of the miracle but there has not been enough focus on hard work to build the ideal society we want to become. Our boasting about 'unity in diversity', as set out in our national constitution, will become increasingly hollow over time as many children grow up with no exposure to the diversity of language and culture that is so uniquely enriching in South Africa.

Multilingualism is not just an ideal. It is a necessity in our increasingly interconnected and competitive world. The facility to sing and speak multiple languages and express our multifaceted cultures with passion is our comparative advantage over many in our competitive global community. Why give it up?

CHAPTER 2

NEGOTIATING CULTURE, TRADITIONS AND CUSTOMS IN A DEMOCRACY

There is a need to engage openly in conversations about how we negotiate the minefield of respecting culture and traditions in a constitutional democracy with a diversity of cultures. How do we learn about one another's cultures and how do we critique the continued practices of traditions and customs that undermine the basic tenets of our constitution?

Transmitting the wisdom embedded in cultural practices, traditions and customs is an injunction given to every generation in almost all cultures to ensure that their children do not grow up rootless. My language, Sepedi, is clear on this subject: *Ruta bana ditaola, o se ye natso badimong* (teach insights into the secrets of life to your children; you are not to take them with you when you depart to the land of ancestors). I am emboldened by this injunction to enter this minefield.

Greece, the land of the gods, has of late been in the media for the wrong reasons. In many ways, Greek society lives in another era. In Delphi, for instance, one experiences walking in the footsteps of history – reliving antiquity – yet the ruins of the Temple of Apollo sit comfortably with the goings-on in the life of Delphi in the twenty-first century. One can almost hear the Oracle announcing the do's and don'ts of life as directed by the gods. But the small number of tourists in 2010 when I visited this rich heritage area reminded one of the realities of life in the aftermath of the global financial meltdown.

Greece's financial troubles burst into the consciousness of a people who have by and large led a charmed life. Yet many Greeks seem to remain steadfast in their belief that the troubles of state finances would not substantially affect their personal lifestyles. After all, Greece has not only given the world philosophy, mathematics and art as essential elements of human society, but by preserving their language they are able to tap into their roots for inspiration. I was amazed to learn that there are three forms of the Greek language: classical, clean and modern. The classical is essential to understanding the old texts; the clean is used for formal texts, whilst the modern is the popular version for everyday use.

Greece is able to compete in today's world on its own terms because it has retained its links with its roots. It continues to draw on the wisdom of Homer, Socrates and Hippocrates for inspiration. Many Greeks are taking the storms that are washing over their country today their stride because of their sense of history. The strength of Greek culture is a pillar against which they are able to lean in tough times and it emboldens them to know that theirs is a civilisation that remains respected whatever its economic fortunes may be. Greek culture gives it a competitive edge over other Mediterranean countries and is a huge attraction for international tourists.

South Africans can learn a lot about the value of respect for culture as an economic asset, whilst not necessarily accepting being prisoners of culture. It may well be that the overconfidence of the Greek people as members of an ancient civilisation contributes to their lack of urgency in transforming their economy into one that is based on sound fiscal discipline. The culture of non-payment of taxes is so pervasive that one wonders how a modern state can be sustainable without a strong revenue stream in which taxes are an essential element. A member of our travelling team experienced this absurdity when he insisted on being given a receipt for the repair of a puncture to the wheel of his hired car. In the end the garage owner let him go without paying rather than run the risk of issuing a receipt that would complicate his cash-based business that pays little or no tax.

Conversations about culture can easily become highly charged with emotional overtones. In our own society with its legacy of discrimination against sectors of the population and the treatment of their cultures as inferior to others, such conversations are particularly difficult. It is not surprising that one of the biggest fudges of our compromise political settlement was in the area of language. The legacy of the Anglo-Boer War and the successful struggle by Afrikaners to forge their own language and cultural institutions made compromise difficult. Afrikaners knew enough about the value of developing and protecting language and culture in bolstering pride in a people not to give in to any compromise that would undermine what they had accomplished.

Indigenous African languages, small and fragmented, became lost in translation. The notion that a nation can have eleven official languages is so impractical that it could not have been seriously intended. Power politics won over logic and thereby effectively made indigenous African languages marginal in post-apartheid South Africa. The effective monolingualism that has made English the sole medium of communication in political discourse has profound implications for the possibility of effective participation in the political process by poor illiterate people.

One needs only to listen to our public representatives responding inarticulately to questions from journalists in English. Ordinary citizens who should be holding these leaders accountable are often none the wiser after listening to interviews of public officials in the media. If anything, many are moved to empathise with the errant politician as he or she struggles to express themselves in a language that is not their own. One wonders why our politicians do not follow the good example of their peers in many Asian, Latin American and European countries who simply speak in their native languages.

Other aspects of our multicultural society have also been subject to compromise. Issues that come to mind are the coexistence of traditional leadership in a democracy, gender equality and persistence of customary practices, the rights of the child within an authoritarian cultural framework, and so on. Poor rural black people paid the highest price for the compromise settlement, given the negative impact of customary law that remains insensitive to the equality imperatives of our national constitution. Black rural women are the most adversely affected by many of these compromises.

Whatever approach we take in the discussion of culture, traditions and customs, we need to confront the contradictions embedded in our national constitution which sets extremely high standards of conduct for our society – the state, government and civil society. The constitutional democracy we committed to in the basic tenets of our constitution requires behaviour by all parties to be judged by the high standards of human rights and integrity. Few countries have succeeded in living up to these standards.

In addition, the parties expected to perform according to these high standards had no prior experience to guide them, since our legacy as a nation left us ill-prepared for the responsibilities of citizenship in a human rights cultural milieu – the colonial and apartheid systems of government were completely counter to the basic tenets of a human rights culture. Many practices during the anti-apartheid struggle also undermined respect for the human rights of both opponents and comrades who were regarded as sell-outs and many South Africans were caught in the vortex of human rights violations to achieve political ends.

The South African state, constituted by the institutions, both tangible and intangible, that are fundamental to good governance and protection of the constitution, remains a work in progress. The fragility of our state institutions is a function of our legacy of non-democratic governance and the ambivalence of the present actors towards entrenching constitutional democracy. There is still too much confidence in the importance of individuals and political actors as the guarantors of democracy, rather than citizens putting their faith in institutions. The conflation of the state, government, the governing political party and political leaders remains the greatest threat to the entrenchment of our constitutional democracy.

Despite the best efforts of many of its members, the government remains significantly challenged to operate with confidence to meet the high standards set by our constitution and citizens lack the experience to exercise their rights and responsibilities meaningfully and to hold those in authority accountable. Many citizens see themselves as recipients of government largesse rather than as sovereigns who need to take ownership of the resources of the country and ensure that they are well managed. It is not surprising that we are struggling to confront the major contradictions inherent in our constitutional dispensation; we simply do not have the capacity nor, in many cases, the will to tackle them.

I have confidence in your generation to tackle these contradictions. You should be proud that the freedom we enjoy today was fought for largely by young people of previous generations, many of them barely out of their teens. They were inspired by the dream of a society that would respect and accord dignity to human beings simply because of their humanity. At the heart of a dignified life is the control of your own destiny and the confidence that your abilities will be recognised and rewarded fairly. The young people who fought for this freedom did not shun controversy because they understood that social transformation was about disruption of old dysfunctional patterns in order to usher in new ones.

Your responsibilities are greater because many of you are far more educated than earlier generations and have been exposed to the information society of the twenty-first century. You are able to compare and contrast your country's performance with that of others at the same level of development, or better or worse, and to learn the lessons of history. In 2011 it was estimated that the 18 to 35 year age group stands at 37 per cent[12] and you therefore constitute the largest, most active population in our society.

The last decade and a half has seen remarkable changes in our society and your generation and those of your children and grandchildren will be the beneficiaries and embodiments of these changes. Socio-economic change on the scale contemplated in such a short space of time is unusual in world history and you face a huge challenge in refining and completing the process of social transformation. The unfinished agenda is that of ensuring that we can leverage our unity in diversity in a manner that will put us in a much stronger position to create a truly inclusive society. By playing to its strengths, such a society will be more dynamic and economically competitive and will make a more effective contribution to building unity in diversity in our increasingly interconnected global community.

———————

Let us start with language. Parliament, the custodian of laws and policies that give effect to the tenets of our human rights national constitution, pays lip service to respect for the notion of eleven official languages. One hardly hears any language other than English spoken in the National Assembly. The technology for simultaneous translation exists and is used in most international conferences and seminars, but not in our parliament. Promises that parliamentary debates recorded in Hansard (the official record of parliamentary proceedings) would be translated into all official languages remain just that – promises. The only time one is given a real flavour of our multicultural parliament is when members of parliament show off their traditional outfits at the opening of parliament. How, then, should we be talking about and living out our unity in diversity?

Imagine if South Africa could invest in ensuring that all its children learn through the medium of their chosen mother tongue in the first four grades at school. English and another chosen language could be introduced as subjects as early as Grade 1 to be deepened over the years at school. Learning other people's languages is much easier if it is built on a firm foundation of the mother tongue. This is not only because the home language is affirmed for the child on his or her first day at school and communication with parents and other care-givers at home is strengthened, but also because language is a carrier of culture.

Affirmation of children's home culture builds self-confidence because it establishes children's equality alongside those from other cultures. They do not have to apologise for the fact that their name has clicks that the teacher is unable to pronounce, and so the child has to acquiesce to a nickname for the teacher's convenience, or the pronunciation of the name is so distorted that the child feels guilty for making the teacher's life difficult by having a name that is hard to pronounce.

The damage done to our children and grandchildren in this education context is immense. How many times have we heard African language speakers pronounce their own and their peers' names as if they were born and bred in some foreign place? For example, *Ka-ra-bho* instead of Karabo; *Di-mpho* instead of Dimpho; *Thaa-bho* instead of Thabo are names commonly mispronounced by many South Africans, including reporters on our national broadcaster, the South African Broadcasting Corporation (SABC).

The neglect and undermining of African languages unfortunately exacerbates the pain of humiliation that African people suffered over the decades of racist oppression. The wounds of the indignities of the past are unlikely to heal in our lifetime unless we address the issue of language. It is ironic that successive post-apartheid governments have not focused on this question despite the impact language has on sustainable socio-economic transformation. African language speakers, both adults and children, are put at a disadvantage by having to communicate in what is a second or third language for them in an environment in which the English language is equated with general competence and sophistication. Even politicians, who should be setting the tone, have taken to torturing themselves whilst talking to voters, the majority of whom are not first language English speakers. How I long to see our president speaking eloquently in isiZulu at the UN or at the G20 as East Asian presidents tend to do.

Monolingualism impoverishes societies that practise it. Why should South African children, who have such a rich heritage, be left with such limited language competence? Children everywhere demonstrate an amazing capacity to learn multiple languages. I have friends who have taught their children the mother tongues of both parents in addition to whatever the language requirements of their school systems are. The mother consistently speaks to the children in Afrikaans, Arabic, Greek or Swedish whilst the father also uses his mother tongue consistently when talking to them. These children not only thrive but excel.

One of the fundamental errors of our society is to underestimate our own as well as our children's capacity for excellence. We settle for less because we are nervous about setting high expectations for ourselves lest we fail and prove our detractors right. The unspoken fear of failure which would confirm the worst racial stereotypes about black inferiority and white superiority has held us captive to a downward spiral of tolerance for mediocrity. We refuse to challenge one another to perform at the highest levels because we do not want to expose ourselves to scrutiny by those who might judge us negatively. Teachers, nurses, government officials and those in the private sector conspire in the promotion of a culture of mediocrity in the name of solidarity and it is our children who are the ultimate losers.

The underperformance of our education system, especially at the level where proper foundations for learning how to learn are supposed to be laid, is in part due to inappropriate language policies. The notion that parents who have been conditioned to believe in the superiority of the English language can elect to have their children taught through the medium of their mother tongue, is fundamentally flawed. Many of you as educated professionals have possibly opted for English medium instruction for your own children because you believe that it will give them a head start in life. But, as has been demonstrated internationally, mother tongue instruction in the foundation phase is what will give them a head start. That choice forces us to double our efforts to support our children in their language development. We need to have serious public debates on this issue before it is too late.

To add insult to injury, the quality of English that is being taught in our school system has been deliberately lowered to reduce the risk of failure for the majority of children. Gone are the days of classical texts in all languages that tested pupils' capacities. Gone are the long reading lists that exposed pupils to poetry, prose and novels that stimulated their appreciation of language. Our children and grandchildren graduate from high school without the necessary preparation for life in an interconnected world where language competence is critical. Results of a Higher Education of South Africa (HESA) study on the competence of the 2009 high school graduates who entered higher education provide a damning testimony to the impact of this language policy. In 2010, only 50 per cent of students entering higher education for the first time had adequate literacy to tackle the challenges of academia. Only seven per cent had mathematical competence at the appropriate level. How does one teach at the tertiary level from such a low base of literacy and numeracy?

The more than half a million graduates of the Class of 2010 will sadly add to the now nearly four million (and growing) frustrated young people who have not been able to enter employment or further training because of poor educational preparation. So low are our expectations of our children that we celebrate a pass rate of 68 per cent as acceptable. To make matters worse, the hurdle is set so low that the majority of those who have succeeded need only achieve 30 per cent in three subjects and 40 per cent in three others to qualify for a pass – this in an education system that is so wasteful that less than half of the original cohort of 1.3 million who started school in 1999 ended up writing the final matriculation examinations. Only about 20 per cent of this cohort qualified for higher education.

In most successful societies it is accepted across time and space that parents expect and ensure that their offspring and the following generations will do better than they themselves did. Progress and prosperity are measured by how much better younger generations do than their predecessors. How come, then, that we as citizens of post-apartheid South Africa seem to have lowered our expectations of what our children and grandchildren can achieve in many walks of life? My generation had to obtain a minimum of 50 per cent to pass any subject or grade and much higher than that to gain university entrance. Many of us had parents who, despite their own low levels of education, pushed us to achieve at the level of excellence. Fifty per cent was regarded as mediocre – 'madoda score'.

Post-apartheid South Africa is presiding over the death of indigenous African languages. Not only are mother tongue indigenous African language children not learning their own languages, but schools have over the last sixteen years been increasingly abandoning efforts to teach indigenous languages to their pupils. They argue that the curriculum is too difficult for their pupils, including mother tongue speakers, to get good grades. The focus on grades rather than the value of learning is leading to fewer students opting to take these languages – and there are no disincentives for opting out.

Can you imagine graduating from high school in France or Germany without competence in those languages? In fact those countries insist that even as foreign students one has to learn the language before engaging in the content studies one is committed to. Studying engineering in Germany comes with learning the German language. Similarly, French language is essential to benefiting from postgraduate studies in France. Sadly, the African languages are treated as dispensable in our own country and the long-term costs of this are likely to be immense. Recent attempts by the Department of Basic Education to reverse this trend are welcome, but a much greater effort will be needed to undo the damage of the last few decades of neglect.

Our children need to be read to and to have storytelling sessions with older generations to learn to enjoy and imagine the world in their mother tongue. Storytelling is also a wonderful medium for cross-generation communication. Gcina Mhlophe, a well-known storyteller who lives in Durban and performs worldwide, should be on SABC Radio and TV

every day to demonstrate the power of her storytelling and the
isiZulu in this. She is able to take children into the world of fo
African wisdom and philosophy are effortlessly transmitted through
animal stories, the famous ones being about how small animals outwit
big ones by playing to their strengths as more nimble and innovative.
For example, how an ant in the trunk of an elephant can make the giant
of the wilderness so irritated that it may lose its sanity. Or how the hare
out-foxes the fox by playing to the latter's weaknesses. Gcina's daughter
is blessed to be able to travel with her mother and to share this wisdom.
Hers is an inspired life enriched by the art of storytelling.

Contrast this with many of our children and grandchildren who
spend much of their free time glued to television sets. We should not
be surprised that many of these children cannot read, write or reason
well. Their mental, social and physical development is impaired by the
lack of challenge to their imagination and their bodies. Storytelling
is an active process that requires the participation of both performer
and listener, whereas TV programmes are passive signals requiring no
active engagement on the part of the listener. In many TV programmes
nothing much is left to the imagination and so there is little challenge to
the developing mind.

My great-grandmother had a foolproof tactic to keep us actively
listening to her stories. We were required to punctuate segments of the
story with affirmations that we were following the narrative by saying
'Keleketla' (meaning *I am listening*). As we became drowsier we would
fall silent and she would then rouse us and direct us to bed. Those were
idyllic times. My great-grandmother understood the responsibilities
of intergenerational conversations and the sharing of knowledge and
wisdom. The critical issue with respect to such conversations is time –

quality time together as families. The equivalent of bedtime storytelling in literary societies is bedtime reading.

It is amazing how few parents spend time on this task despite evidence that indicates that children who are read to grow up loving to read and do better not just in languages but in their capacity to imagine, read with comprehension and express themselves confidently. In our multilingual society promoting a reading culture is essential to generating interest in languages and other cultures that children would encounter in their reading or being read to. South Africa has to turn its challenges of having to live up to its commitment to respect all eleven official languages into an opportunity to become a laboratory where best practice is developed in multilingualism.

I am not for a moment suggesting that promoting eleven official languages will be easy. We missed the moment during the negotiation process of settling for one Nguni and one Sesotho language as the languages to be promoted in our education system, depending on which province people lived in. Julius Nyerere, the first president of Tanzania, managed to bind the Tanzanian nation together by promoting unity through the use of KiSwahili and English as official languages. It was not a popular decision, but he considered it the right thing to do to reduce the risks of tribalism and to build a united nation loyal only to Tanzania. He succeeded, showing us that inspirational and courageous leadership is essential for major social transformation processes.

We look to your generation to contribute to debates and actions to address this critical area of our social life. It begins with your conduct as a member of your family and your relationships with siblings, intimate partners, spouses and offspring, as well as your conduct as a professional in the workplace and wider community. Do you model the idealism embedded in our national constitution?

Traditional leadership is the second area of unfinished business of the transformation agenda. The compromise of retaining traditional leadership structures in the governance of our constitutional democracy has had serious consequences for rural people, many of whom are poor black women. Local authorities in any governance system are the locus of execution on promises of public services to meet basic needs and the stronger the system of local authority, the more likely are public services to be of high quality. But our local authority system is undermined by the dominance of political party influence in determining who gets on to the list and in what order in the proportional representation electoral system. The weak electoral constituency system in our democracy renders communities largely powerless to hold their local authority officials accountable for quality performance.

The party list system is a cancer in our political structure. It tilts the scales of accountability too far in favour of party leaders who determine who occupies what position on the list, regardless of the views of those affected by their performance in office. Traditional leadership structures superimposed on such a weak accountability system in rural areas is a recipe for growing inequality between urban and rural areas. It is an additional burden for poor rural people to bear simply in order to sustain our compromise democratic settlement.

The May 2010 ruling by the Constitutional Court struck down the 2004 Communal Land Rights Act No. 11 signed into law by President Thabo

Mbeki. The Court was emphatic in declaring 'the entire Act invalid because it was not adopted in terms of the correct procedure prescribed by the Constitution'. The judge argued that various provisions of the Communal Land Rights Act affect, in substantial measure, indigenous law and traditional leadership, which are areas of concurrent national and provincial competence. The law sought to entrench the power of traditional leaders to allocate land in areas under their jurisdiction, such allocations often being arbitrary, nepotistic, corrupt and heavily loaded against women. The patriarchal nature of much of traditional leadership undermines the gender equality tenets of our constitution and the discriminatory nature of the application of the law in certain communities goes against the grain of the equality principle at the heart of the constitution.

How could parliament have overlooked the unconstitutionality of this law? Did it neglect its duty as watchdog and upholder of the constitution? Why did this happen when our parliament has more women MPs than most others on our continent? Did party political interests trump the watchdog role? Where was the Gender Commission in all this? Did it blow the whistle or was it sleeping at the wheel? What about ordinary citizens who are the ultimate stewards of our democracy and its human rights standards?

My own family has been a victim of this unconstitutional law. My father, his siblings and some members of the extended Ramphele family invested in buying land close to the banks of the Lephalale River in an area known as Ga-Seleka in the 1950s. We have title to this land and at great cost won a North Gauteng High Court case in 2009 to evict a squatter who had built a house on our plot despite being warned not to do so. The local chief refused to allow the police to execute the High

Court order on the basis that it was his prerogative to allocate land to whomever he chose and he sided with this particular squatter. We now have to incur additional costs to enforce the Court order. How many families have the resources to fight such battles in remote rural areas? Political expediency by the then government and a compliant parliament has denied poor rural people equality in the law and enjoyment of the freedom to access opportunities to enhance their livelihoods.

Another example is the abuse of power by chiefs to capture communal resources in areas under their jurisdictions. In Ncora in the Cofimvaba district near Queenstown, for example, an irrigation system established in 1976 by Kaizer Matanzima, leader of the then Transkei Bantustan, remains unused despite the millions of rands invested in it. The revitalisation process of this irrigation scheme in 2000 was undermined by a local chief who excluded the communities who had worked the land, but were denied the benefit of the produce. Collective investment of time and energy by ordinary rural folk had resulted in outstanding produce which was summarily captured by the local chief for his benefit alone. The sad reality is that those poor folk have no one to help them fight the case.

The claim that the land belonged to the chief could not have stood the test of even traditional customary law. Communal land, according to custom and tradition, is held in trust by chiefs who are to ensure that the needs of those living and working the land are protected and that justice prevails. But both the provincial and national governments are loath to challenge traditional leaders for fear of losing their loyalty and, with it, the votes of the people under their authority. Needless to say, the Ncora Project collapsed again a decade ago. Only collective action based on respect for the rights of each citizen can succeed in resuscitating and sustaining such projects.

There is a cruel irony in the promotion of traditional authority structures at the expense of citizens in rural areas. The system of traditional leadership was regarded by those fighting for freedom across the ideological spectrum as largely corrupted by the divide and rule tactics of successive white governments. The payment of chiefs by those governments was at the heart of this corruption. Instead of chiefs being rewarded by their own people for promoting prosperity for all, as had been the practice of traditional systems prior to colonial conquest, today's payment of chiefs is unrelated to performance. The wisdom of traditional practice in aligning the incentives of chiefs to those of their people to ensure shared prosperity has been discarded in favour of an entitlement system for the chiefs in exchange for their loyalty to the party in government.

Are we surprised that traditional leaders have become so demanding of ever more benefits regardless of the negative impact of such demands on the national budget? In the Eastern Cape, poor rural communities are often at the mercy of traditional leaders who make no pretence of meeting the needs of ordinary people. We rely on your generation to reopen the debate on the place of traditional leadership in a constitutional democracy so that it is realigned with the tenets of our national constitution. Respecting traditional authorities need not come at the expense of poor rural communities; we need to challenge the approach that makes them bear a disproportionate burden of the costs of our political compromise.

Traditional authorities are bound like the rest of us by the tenets of our national constitution which demands equality before the law for everybody and they should be held to account if they violate the socio-economic rights of poor people that are entrenched in our Bill of Rights. Their right to practise traditional leadership has to be linked to the responsibilities that flow from their positions to promote the progressive realisation of the socio-economic rights of their fellow citizens in the areas under their authority.

There are, fortunately, progressive traditional leaders such as the Royal Bafokeng authorities. They outwitted the apartheid government and the mining industry by securing mineral rights and protecting them from the negative impact of the Minerals Act of 1991 passed in 1992 that excluded surface land right owners from any claim on the right to the minerals discovered underground. This Act was most probably sponsored by key players in the mining industry to protect their unfettered access to mineral resources in anticipation of the transition to democracy. The Royal Bafokeng tribe fought for and retained their right to negotiate with private exploration and mining companies.

Under Chief Leruo, the Royal Bafokeng are harnessing the platinum mineral wealth in the belly of the earth on their land to promote sustainable development of communities in the areas of the North West Province under their control. They have placed huge emphasis on education as a priority for investment, recognising that education is the sure and tested route out of poverty, and they have appointed experts to review and strengthen education at all levels for the benefit of the Bafokeng people. The Royal Bafokeng authorities have demonstrated that there is no necessary contradiction between traditional leadership and respect for and promotion of human rights and sustainable development.

---

ler equality is perhaps the biggest cultural challenge of our times. We have left the hunter and gatherer social environment behind us, yet we remain prisoners of its logic in the way we allocate roles to men and women. Hunting required the physique to run and the muscular strength that is characteristic of the male side of the species. Women's bodies are not physiologically or anatomically geared to sustain high intensity physical demands such as hunting; they are designed for conception, gestation, birthing and the nurturing of offspring. Their gathering roles best suited their reproductive and nurturing roles since they took place in the proximity of their homes and were less physically demanding than the hunting done by men. But time has moved on. Hunting and gathering roles can today be undertaken by either men or women and earning a livelihood is not the monopoly of either.

The South African Institute of Race Relations' Labour Participation figures show that in 2010 54 per cent of economically active citizens were employed. Of these, 62 per cent were men and 48 per cent were women. Amongst white women, 61 per cent of those economically active were in employment versus 45 per cent amongst Africans and 58 per cent amongst those classified Coloured. There is a higher level of unemployment amongst women than men and amongst African people versus other cultural groups.[13] The lag in labour participation by women is also reflected in the under-representation of women in top management. In 2008 men made up 82 per cent of top management with white women dominating the female representation at 76 per cent versus only 24 per cent representation by black women.[14] It is clear that notwithstanding policies affirming gender equality and emphasis on achieving it in the provisions of numerous legislations, progress has been slow. Women still lag in their exercise of economic power and influence in major business enterprises.

Cultural transformation in this domain faces many obstacles. The difference between men and women is functional to sustaining society so that they can live in a complementary way, but in almost all cultures it has been codified into role differentiations that have come to be seen as immutable. Real men are not supposed to do this or that, especially in the domestic arena. Nurturing roles belong to women and real men dare not be seen feeding babies or, heaven forbid, changing nappies.

I am very proud when I see some of my sons and daughters finding the right balance between time for themselves as lovers/married couples, sharing nurturing roles and supporting each other in their professional roles. It is not easy, but it can be done if the focus is not competition but complementarity. Most women are better suited than their male partners to being the primary nurturer and care-giver for the children. Smart couples support this by ensuring that the man is inducted into sharing as much as possible of the really tough, stressful aspects.

I had the good fortune of being brought up by women who were professional multi-taskers, seamlessly occupying positions as wife, mother, professional and community leader. They leveraged the power derived from one domain to tackle the others. For example my mother, as a Grade 1 teacher, was respected by other women as a competent home-maker and she used that position to lead the community in home-making skills, nutrition and child care to improve the well-being of the community as a whole. Being a professional also meant that her expertise as a cook and event organiser elevated her to the level of community leader beyond her village. It was striking how my mother and grandmothers carried their multiple roles so effortlessly. My grandmother would be praise-singing and babysitting at the same time, while my mother would breast-feed at school during the short break.

They were unselfconscious about each role they played.

I have tried in my own way to learn from this in discharging my roles as mother, grandmother, professional, leader and citizen. I enjoy the sense of freedom just to be MaMokoena when I visit my home village in Uitkyk No. 1, Bochum, Polokwane in the Limpopo province every year during the Easter long weekend since my mother's passing in 2008. When I get there I switch the frame of language to Sepedi, the pace to slow, and the style to just being. My elder sister Mashadi and I assume my mother's role of ensuring that the home runs smoothly for the four generations gathered there. My brothers slaughter a sheep from the flock my sister has built up over the last three years, we bake bread and cook delicacies, we play and chat and laugh with our grandchildren. We just have a good time with each person playing to his or her strengths. I draw my inspiration and passion for life from this seamless transition from the high professional life and global encounters to village life with its unhurried rhythm. My grandson and my business colleagues are a continuum of the human connectedness that I live as a daily reality.

You have to find your own way. There is no set formula for social relationships, given their deep spiritual foundations and expressions. No two spirits take the same route to finding the peace that only manifests from a profound sense of being in harmony with the self. You must not torture yourself by trying to be like your peers. You have to find what works for you within the value framework you choose to govern your life at the personal, professional and political levels. Finding that harmony is key to happiness and self-actualisation.

Unfortunately, life is more complex than this. There are also differences between men as well as between women in the sensitive arena of sexuality. We now know enough biology and physiology to understand that the human species expresses a variety of sexual orientations, yet the criminalisation of homosexual and lesbian relationships persists. The assertion is that it is not in our culture to have people engage in such sexual relationships. In Uganda this attitude resulted in the brutal murder early in 2011 of a campaigner for freedom of expression of human sexuality, and in Malawi a gay couple was jailed in 2010 for daring to commit publicly to living together as a couple bound by love.

It is true that for the older generation which grew up in conservative cultural environments, without exposure to the realities of the varied expression of human sexuality, coming to terms with open expression of this variation may be difficult. My late mother, who was well travelled and well read, battled to come to terms with this reality but she made peace with it when I pointed out that some of my friends whom she loved were either lesbians or gay men. She had to readjust her lens which had been framed by prejudice against gay and lesbian people as 'abnormal'. Having got to meet and like them as my friends, she could not sustain the 'abnormality' tag.

Your generation has both the opportunity and the responsibility presented by living in an African country that has stretched its idealism to recognise and protect the rights of all people, including those with sexual orientations other than heterosexuality, to develop your capacity to confront and protect the human rights of such people. It is appalling that as a society founded on a human rights constitution we can tolerate the abuse of lesbians through so-called corrective rape and murder in the name of African culture. There are no firm statistics of these crimes, but one high profile case was that of a woman soccer player from Khayelitsha who was murdered because she was a lesbian.

here was the case of a young woman who was brutally assaulted nale cousin who took it upon himself to beat her up and rape her. Her relatives were aware of the assault because they heard her screams, but none came to her rescue, leaving her completely at the mercy of her assailant who regarded it as a matter of honour to discipline her out of her lesbian orientation. She subsequently died and her assailant is out on token bail and proud of the honour killing he committed. Neither the law enforcement system nor the judicial system has demonstrated intolerance for this despicable crime against women. Indeed, law enforcement officers have been found to be both tardy and reluctant to react in such cases. Nor have our political, civic and private sector leaders taken action against this behaviour which is nothing less than a crime against humanity for which we should display zero tolerance.

The tolerance of human rights abuse extends beyond those seen as 'other'. It colours relationships within homes, communities and wider society. The level of violence goes beyond the need to dominate; its brutality is indicative of the turmoil in the mind of the perpetrators. The epidemic of violence against women and children is emblematic of a society at war with itself, a symptom of the poisonous wounds in the spirit of the nation. Both men and women are caught up in this brutality, but men are more often than not the perpetrators. Why?

I firmly believe that our patriarchal culture put inordinate pressures on men to perform roles beyond their capabilities. The provider role requires skills and experience that are not available to many young men in our society. The underperformance of our education and training systems has left many 18 to 35-year-olds without the capability of earning sustainable livelihoods. Public service jobs require basic minimum qualifications unattainable by most. A significant proportion of those who are fortunate enough to have political connections forge their qualifications to get high-paying jobs, but for the majority there is no hope.

The 2009 Dinokeng Scenarios Report showed that in 2008 there were nearly three million young people in the age group 18 to 24 years who were not in school, not in training and not working. That figure reached four million in 2011. According to the National Planning Commission Report, unemployment amongst 15 to 24-year-olds was at 51 per cent in 2010.[15] Talented young people who have been unable to find employment are likely to be very angry at the society that has failed them. Many end up as petty criminals or substance abusers who graduate into brutal addicts and many will commit heinous crimes within their own families and communities as well as in the wider society, and often those close to them in their homes and communities will become their victims. Grandmothers, mothers and sisters become the target of the rage of frustrated young men.

It does not help that these young men not only have few opportunities but are also unlikely to have positive male role models. They operate outside accepted norms and values because many raised themselves. Society abandoned them and consequently they feel no obligation towards society. Some of the patterns of substance abuse suggest suicidal tendencies – how else does one explain the emerging pattern of smoking dagga mixed with ARVs and rat poison? How is it possible that battery acid can be seen as an appropriate ingredient to boost the potency of alcoholic drinks? South Africa is witnessing a destruction of its human capital base, but we do not seem to realise that this is a crisis because many of us have insulated ourselves from the areas where this catastrophe is being played out.

Middle and upper middle-class black people moved out of poor communities in droves after 1994. Opportunities that are open to those with education and training have created a brain drain from the townships and rural areas and the problem is exacerbated by the persistence of apartheid's geography under the watch of successive post-apartheid governments. Mixed residential housing that enables poor young people to grow up in neighbourhoods where they can see lawyers, teachers, nurses and other professionals in regular employment is critical if their horizons are to be broadened. The cycle of multigenerational unemployment simply breeds hopelessness.

Young women too bear many burdens. Increasing sexual assault, often by relatives, including their own fathers or teachers, is often borne in silence. Teenage pregnancy is high as is the prevalence of HIV/AIDS. Caring for dying relatives and younger siblings is becoming a common feature in the lives of young women, some of them barely ten years old, and poverty and hunger are the daily companions of many. They also lack positive role models and the notion of gender equality remains a distant dream in the battle just to stay alive.

Your generation has both the opportunity and responsibility to turn this situation around. You are the older brothers and sisters, uncles and aunts, and professional practitioners – the teachers, nurses, lawyers and public officials – who can and should reach out to this generation at risk. This is where intergenerational conversations, knowledge sharing, modelling appropriate behaviour and mentoring across class and culture will have huge returns for you as individuals because you will be enriched by touching the lives of others and helping to heal them.

Your generation presents an opportunity for society to reinvent itself by demonstrating that it cares about the welfare of young people and is willing and able to invest in their success so that the 'unity in diversity' enjoined by our constitution can become a reality. Investments in nurturing and promoting the capabilities of the next generation are in the enlightened self-interest of all of society and social stability and sustainable prosperity are not possible without them.

CHAPTER 3

WHAT SYSTEM OF VALUES ARE WE TO LIVE BY?

Shifting the ground of reason has to start with clarity about what our shared values are. The focus on defining success largely in material terms seems to have blinded us to the values that inspired my generation, and those who went before us, in pursuing the struggle to be a free people. We seem to have lost our way in less than two decades of our journey as a young democracy.

Ismail Serageldin, who presented the 2011 Mandela Lecture, defined why values are critical:

> Values create communities out of individuals. Values enable transactions to take place and bridge the inter-generational divide. Values

are what make human society worthy of the designation 'human'. We
have come to rely on our educational system to reinforce what parents
do at home in nurturing the correct values in their growing children.
In the educational system, values are forged by teacher example and
student practice.[16]

Values define who we are as societies. Nothing matters more in life than
clarity on shared values in homes, families, communities and the wider
society. As Serageldin indicates, values make it possible to have common
assumptions as a basis for transactions as individuals with all others. The
centrality of the education system is clearly spelt out as a key institution
in shaping growing young minds to become worthy members of society.
A dysfunctional education system undermines human development
in any society and in our young democracy it also undermines the
inculcation of the values of our founding principles as a society.

Values define the boundaries we set for what we regard as appropriate
behaviour, practices and attitudes. However successful you may be
as young professionals, business people, artists, politicians, or even if
you are unemployed, life becomes a game of chance without a clearly
understood and predictable shared framework of values within which
social relationships may be conducted. Societies nurture and socialise
their offspring to conduct themselves appropriately within shared value
systems through rewarding appropriate behaviour and punishing or
discouraging bad behaviour.

It is necessary for nations to engage in transitions from old to new value
systems as they move from one socio-economic and political system
to another. South Africa recognised the importance of undertaking a
deliberate process of transition from the old ways of racial, class and

gender discrimination towards a more inclusive and equitable system. A fundamental platform for such a transition is setting the ground rules and a shared value system to govern public life and interpersonal relationships between citizens, and to manage shared resources.

We also recognised the importance of tackling the challenge of creating a coherent shared system of values to guide post-apartheid social relationships. Our national constitution accordingly sets out a system of values based on basic universal human rights to provide a framework for our multicultural society to mould itself into a nation that is united in its diversity. Rights and responsibilities are clearly spelt out for us in that founding document to guide our conduct as citizens and as a nation.

A crucial question, however, is the extent to which our founding documents and the values they espouse have been incorporated into our social relationships as well as our way of life and our conduct as citizens. I wonder how many of you have read and understood what we as a nation signed up for in our constitution? How many of you take time to reflect on the values we agreed to live by that feature so prominently in the constitution? How do they guide your daily lives and practices? Understanding, respecting and advancing the precepts of our national constitution is critical to the transition we need to make from the old to the new South Africa.

In addition, South Africans pride themselves as a people who live by the precepts of *Ubuntu* which we love to claim as unique cultural attributes that set Africans apart from people of other cultures. Interconnectedness is at the centre of our being and consciousness as people and *Ubuntu* is an affirmation of that interconnectedness which acknowledges our human dignity by fellow human beings. It is an essential source of meaning and energy to engage life as individuals and communities.

Most Bantu languages in South Africa capture this interconnectedness in metaphors and idioms that place *Ubuntu* at the heart of being human. It is said that 'so and so *ungumtu mpela*' (he or she is a real person), meaning that this person's humaneness shines through everything he or she does. For those who go astray, '*ungumtu onjane na?*' (what kind of person are you?), is a cry of anguish by parents or close relatives who cringe at bad behaviour by one of their own. Some might add: '*Batho ba tla reng na?*' (what will decent people say about your behaviour?). In other words, a person is not only known as a person by virtue of being human; it is of equal importance that he or she behaves in ways defined by the given community as appropriate for his or her age and standing in society.

African cultures are not the only ones founded on the understanding of the deep connectedness of human beings and our interconnected world has exposed us to the importance of being open to learning from others. We are becoming increasingly aware that many other cultures share a similar philosophical orientation. For example, the Japanese call it *ameru* – the 'meeting place' or intersection of all human relationships. Chief Seattle, a Native American, characterised our connectedness as follows:

> Humankind has not woven the web of life. We are but one thread within it. Whatever we do to the web, we do to ourselves. All things are bound together. All things connect.

It is significant that in this formulation, it is not only human beings who are connected, but all of creation as well. Sustainable development and stewardship of our environment take on a new meaning – a matter of preserving ourselves and other creatures with whom we share this world.

Agrarian societies all over the world evolved into understanding that respecting the dignity of other human beings with whom one shares common resources and challenges is essential to sustaining a coherent, stable and mutually respectful community. Lessons from studies of the 'tragedy of the commons' establish beyond doubt the unsustainability of ignoring the need to find a shared understanding of the interdependence of human communities.[17] Richard Wilkinson makes a compelling case that:

> The quality of our relations with other people has always been so crucial not only to wellbeing, but also to survival and to reproductive success, that social interaction has been one of the most powerful influences on the evolution of the human brain.[18]

The Afrikaner community prides itself on a culture that traditionally sets great store in close-knit relationships within the *volk*. In the same way that Africans embrace older people as *uMama, uTata, uMalome, uTat'omkhulu, uMakhulu, uButi, uSisi* and so on, Afrikaners have their *Oom, Tant, Broer, Suster*. The main difference between the Afrikaner approach and *Ubuntu* has historically been the exclusionary nature of relationships within the apartheid-tainted Afrikaner culture that counted white people as the only ones worthy of inclusion. The ideology of the chosen *volk* versus the 'other' undermined what could have been accepted as an Afrikaans cultural expression of *Ubuntu*. The opportunity now is for you, my daughters and sons, to establish a new generational linkage of Afrikaners, Africans, Asian descendants and others to recapture the values embedded in our collective cultural heritage of the inextricable interconnectedness of people as the defining element of being human.

The challenge we face after more than a decade and a half of adopting a human rights-based national constitution is how to close the gap between the value system we committed ourselves to and our actual day to day practices in our social, political and economic relationships. These challenges are more acute for your generation because you do not have the excuse of pleading ignorance. The home, community, workplace and wider society are the arenas where our system of values should find expression – where *Ubuntu* and human rights become the standards against which we measure ourselves. How do we measure up?

Let me remind you of the principles we agreed to and spelt out in our national constitution:

- Human dignity, the achievement of equality and the advancement of human rights and freedoms
- Non-racialism and non-sexism
- Supremacy of the constitution and the rule of law
- Universal adult suffrage, a common national voters roll, regular elections and a multiparty system of democratic government to ensure accountability, responsiveness and openness

These values reflect the idealism which is the foundation of the kind of society we want to build in post-apartheid South Africa, an idealism that is inspired by our cultural heritage of the recognition that our own humanity depends on these respectful relationships with others. Our idealism is reinforced by alignment with the Universal Charter of Human Rights.

We have gone a long way towards living these ideals at various levels of our society in both the private and public spheres. Think of the institutions we have built and the policies we have adopted during the last eighteen years. In many areas they have placed us among the best in promoting the progressive attainment of socio-economic rights. Our country is recognised as the number one in 97 national budget systems evaluated in terms of transparency and we have one of the most progressive and effective tax collection systems in the free world after starting from a very poor base in 1994.

We committed to social justice as a foundation of our society and have succeeded in closing the gap between the allocation of resources on the basis of the colour-coded system of the past to a more equitable needs-based system. We have a Financial and Fiscal Commission (FFC) dedicated to ensuring equity of distribution of resources between and amongst provinces to promote redress of the skewed development that tended to neglect poor, rural and vulnerable communities. We have a well-managed public finance system and a respected Reserve Bank that can hold its head high in the competitive global environment of the twenty-first century. We have a highly respected independent judiciary that has been resilient in the face of numerous challenges from both the left and right over the last eighteen years.

There are, however, serious gaps between the ideals and the reality in our performance. At the heart of our underperformance are failures to translate the values we committed to into the practice of governance that will make freedom a reality in the lives of all citizens. The public service is the machinery that is designed to execute the dreams of our nation and the constitutional provisions envisage a public service imbued with the founding values of our democracy in addition to having the competence and commitment to serve with distinction. Ours was to be a meritocratic public service that exemplified the dawn of a caring government that put people at the centre of the governance process. The public service is not only expected to implement agreed policies and programmes but to create an appropriate environment for the private sector and civil society to contribute to national development goals.

It is against the above values that we should measure the performance of our public service. Of great concern are chronic problems of inefficiency and maladministration in the poorest provinces, such as the Eastern Cape, Mpumalanga, KwaZulu-Natal, Limpopo and Free State. Tragically, the most dysfunctional social sectors are those that impact most directly on poor citizens. The failure to utilise allocated resources to build new and strengthen old infrastructure has robbed them of the benefits of participating in the socio-economic development opportunities that freedom has made possible. These failures represent a denial of freedom for the majority of people in our society and are a betrayal of our values-based national constitution.

Every year billions of unspent funds are returned to the Treasury because of the failure of the public service to execute programmes that were planned and agreed to. For instance, in the 2007-2008 National Financial Year R2 435 309 was returned to the Treasury unspent; the amount was R3 480 999 for the 2008-2009 National Financial Year, and R6 583 059 for the 2009-2010 National Financial Year. The budget allocations for 2011, 2012 and 2013 are R54 462 844, R62 592 908 and R68 837 328 respectively.[19]

Failure to address the inherited disparities in the social sectors has had even more devastating consequences for poor people. Our failure as a society to ensure that every child and young person is given the opportunity to develop into the best he or she can become could be regarded as a crime against humanity. The issue is not one of lack of material resources to develop excellent education, health and welfare systems; the issue is one of failure of leadership at all levels: the government, the teachers, health and welfare professionals, and the private sector. It is the failure to live up to the values that reflect the social justice that we committed to at the dawn of our democracy.

Our failure to make social justice a reality in our democracy demands that we pause and take time to tease out an understanding of why we have not lived up to our commitments, especially given our considerable resources in both the public and private sectors. South Africa is also blessed in having human and intellectual resources that have been recognised in many fields of science and technology, and we also have the ability to tackle complex socio-political matters. We defied naysayers and managed to overcome narrow interests, making possible a historic transition to democracy in the dying days of the twentieth century. What, then, has created the impediments to living our dream?

We need to take a hard look at the choices we made as a democracy and see whether they have helped or impeded the realisation of what we envisaged: a democratic society united in its diversity.

Let us turn to a conversation about choices and the place and role of ethics and morality. Freedom is about the right and the ability to make choices in life and this was the right we won in 1994 when we instituted a system of participatory democracy that would reflect and promote the will of ordinary people to govern. We need to have open discussions about how we understand issues of ethics and morality and how they are reflected in our decision-making framework and the workings of our society.

In his story *The Wages of Synergy*, Theodore Sturgeon[20] raised important questions that may be helpful to our conversations as a society wrestling with how to develop a shared system of values and how to align our decision making at the personal, professional and societal levels. His was a different era, the mid-twentieth century, but his concerns are of relevance today. He asserted that 'an act can be both moral and ethical. But under certain circumstances a moral act can be counter to ethics, and an ethical act can be immoral.' Issues of morality are often associated with group survival. Groups – whether they be families, communities, religious or other institutions – often elaborate codes of conduct that ensure that members behave in ways that do not violate agreed norms. Such norms form the basis of what is and isn't acceptable as appropriate behaviour, which in turn defines what is moral and immoral. Examples are taboos on marrying siblings or offspring, obedience to one's parents and elders, observing certain rituals, and so on. Ethics, on the other hand, offers frames of reference that individuals may use to make choices and to distinguish between what they consider good or evil. It is possible for ethical imperatives to stand in conflict with moral obligations, which presents us with serious dilemmas. Does one follow one's conscience even if it conflicts with the norms of one's community or society?

Carl Jung, the renowned psychoanalyst, felt very strongly that human beings cannot escape the torment of ethical decision. He stated boldly that

Harsh as it might sound, we must have the freedom in some circumstances to avoid the known moral good and do what is considered evil, if our ethical decision so requires.[21]

Jung suggests that we should not fall victim to the 'either or' but allow ourselves to resolve 'conflicts of duty' by leaving the ethical choice to the individual. This practice is often invoked in democratic parliaments where members are allowed to vote according to their consciences on difficult issues of 'conflict of duty', such as abortion or euthanasia.

Ethical choices are burning issues of daily life when one has to confront making decisions that go against accepted norms and practices. An extreme example is the mortuary practice which was customary in some ethnic groups in West Africa that involved eating a piece of the flesh of the deceased relative as a moral obligation to ensure the incorporation of past generations into present ones. This moral obligation was not only ethically objectionable, as all cannibalism is, but it also contributed to the spread of serious diseases amongst those involved in consuming flesh infected with life-threatening conditions. Individuals who refused to follow this norm on ethical grounds were regarded by their relatives and community as doing something immoral. How could one refuse to follow traditions that honour the dead and ensure perpetuation of a connection between the dead and the living? It took serious, tough conversations within practising communities and hard work by health professionals over a long period of time to eradicate this practice as an acceptable mortuary ritual.

Ethical stances are hard even in less dramatic areas of life. Does one blow the whistle on a colleague involved in wrong-doing who might, as a result, end up losing his job? The health profession is an arena that is fraught with such ethical dilemmas. Many cases of malpractice are lost for lack of conclusive evidence because colleagues cover up for one another in the name of collegiality. Malpractice statistics show a frightening 900 per cent increase over the last ten years of claims over R5 million and no fewer than two thousand claims in 2010 alone. The same applies to anti-competitive behaviour which thrives on collusion within the particular industries involved. For example, the bread industry has been found to have acted improperly as a cartel colluding in increasing prices of a staple consumed largely by poor people. Here the profit motive led to the major bread-making companies colluding against the interests of poor people – an ethically and morally wrong decision.

I know that many of you struggle with moral and ethical issues in your daily lives. Let us look at the case of Lungile.

Lungile is a young professional in one of our national departments. He is struggling to manage his own performance as an official responsible for establishing, monitoring and ensuring that the procurement processes of the department meet the requirements of the Public Finance Management Act (PFMA). The PFMA sets out very robust criteria of what is and isn't acceptable in terms of the rules under this act. He also has to deal with pressures from one of his senior managers who is insisting that he process a procurement deal that does not meet the requirements. He has been arguing for months that he cannot break the rules. He is then confronted one day by the assistant to the same senior manager telling him that the deal has to be processed under an emergency clause in the Act that provides a waiver to meet urgent needs. What does he do now? The assistant helpfully suggests that Lungile should not put himself at risk when so many others have found this emergency clause a helpful way out of the pressure to allocate deals to politically connected people. Should Lungile not just sign and be free to get on with his work as a dedicated public servant? Lungile is also reminded of those who defied their seniors and ended up seeing the reality of the career-limiting impact of such defiance. Just sign and forget about it, urges his colleague.

How would you respond? Remember that these are not empty threats that Lungile is facing. Nor is the reminder by his colleague an empty threat. There are numerous cases of good performers being frozen out of promotions and whistle blowers being exposed to threats against their lives without any real protection from the legal and judicial systems. Should Lungile take the risk of adding to these statistics? Or should he focus on protecting his career as a good performer and find safe ways out of the ethical dilemmas of being asked to place loyalty to his seniors above propriety as a public servant? If you were Lungile, what would you do?

Solidarity and loyalty become a major cost to the wider society and to the quality of our democracy. Corruption and maladministration are often concealed to protect fellow party members, leading to a culture of impunity. How do honest citizens who are loyal party members respond to the conflict of duty to the party that undermines their duty to the wider nation? Sadly, very few have been willing to break ranks and report wrong-doing and the few who do end up marginalised and may be dismissed from key jobs. There are also increasing numbers of whistle blowers who die mysteriously and little progress is made in the investigation of their deaths. The cost of breaking ranks is high. Ethical choices by honest citizens often put them at loggerheads with party morality that places a premium on loyalty to the party. How do such members resolve these conflicts of duty?

Many young professionals find themselves between a rock and a hard place. Do they follow their ethical inclinations to blow the whistle and ensure that those involved in wrong-doing are held to account, or do they mind their own business and remain quiet? This is a major ethical dilemma as speaking up might be at the cost of one's job and opportunities for advancement in one's career. Remaining quiet might lead to major moral crises for individuals who feel compromised and unable to live with themselves and many end up becoming vulnerable to substance abuse to dull the pain of 'conflicts of duty'. Professionals who are so compromised worry about how to maintain and sustain their integrity in the face of a system that sees integrity as dispensable in favour of political loyalty and solidarity. Public debates on these issues might be helpful to enable those wrestling with such dilemmas to share their anguish and to learn from their peers.

Multiparty democracy demands that citizens be allowed the space to make free choices about their preferred party, representatives and, within their party, what policy directions they would like to promote. The ANC is confronting South Africa as a young democracy with a major moral and ethical dilemma. As a party it prides itself on being disciplined, only allowing disagreements between segments of its membership and/or contestants for leadership to be dealt with internally. This might make sense from the point of view of ensuring coherence of the party machine, but recent history demonstrates that such internal discipline undermines the promotion of democratic practices and free choice by members of the largest party in the country. The intrigues of competition for leadership positions have dominated our politics since 1994 with conflicts derailing the good functioning of government. State organs are often used to support or undermine one or other side. This is particularly worrying when state intelligence agencies enter the fray because of the risks this poses to national security.

The Arms Deal, which continues to fester like a gangrenous sore on the body politic of our young democracy, is a case in point. Members of the ANC in parliament, especially those who were on the Special Committee on Public Accounts (Scopa), found themselves on the horns of this dilemma. Their watchdog responsibilities as members of parliament demanded that they investigate the allegations of corruption, bribery and general flouting of procurement procedures regarding the first arms purchases of post-apartheid South Africa. Their party expected them to follow the line of obstructing any probe into the Arms Deal. Andrew Feinstein decided to resign from parliament rather than follow the party line. He left South Africa for London where he wrote his exposé, *After the Party*,[22] which details the extent to which the process followed to choose the nature of the arms and the suppliers flouted public procurement rules. Others remained within the party, despite their discomfort at acquiescing to a deal which was fatally flawed and extracted opportunity and direct costs the country can hardly afford. The current price tag stands close to R60 billion and it is estimated that it could increase to R70 billion by the time we settle the debt.

The Constitutional Court challenge by economist and activist Terry Crawford-Browne that was due to be heard in November 2011 forced President Zuma to institute a judicial inquiry into the Arms Deal in late October 2011. A panel of three judges led by Judge Willie Seriti of the Supreme Court of Justice has been empowered to investigate all matters related to this blight on our public life and report within two years. There has been widespread acceptance of this as an essential step to clearing the poisonous odour the post-apartheid arms deal has cast over our democracy, fuelling a culture of impunity in public life that has seen corruption rise to frightening levels.

As corruption has spread to poison many other areas of public life, conflict of duty rages on for those party members who would like to see good governance and efficient and effective government performance. Their ethics of fighting corruption is at variance with their moral duties to the ANC which are seen as promoting loyalty and protection of the party and comrades even at the expense of good governance. How sustainable is this ongoing conflict of duty and at what cost does it come to our young democracy? More and more ordinary citizens who are members of the ANC find themselves on the horns of a dilemma – how do they keep voting for a party that, in the words of its own Secretary General, Gwede Mantashe, 'is seen to be soft on corruption'?

Many are former activists with strong ties to the ANC, whilst others remain members because their families or friends are members. It is unthinkable for them *not* to vote for the ANC for this would be a betrayal of loyalty with which they could not live. After all, the ANC is the party of Nelson Rolihlahla Mandela and part of his legacy and how could one betray his legacy by turning one's back on the ANC? How can one preserve the legacy of an icon and his traditional base, the ANC on one hand, and, on the other, discharge one's responsibility to preserve his ideals embedded in the constitutional democracy? How this dilemma is resolved has major implications for the quality and sustainability of our constitutional democracy.

There is a need for open, honest discussion on how one resolves this conflict as an individual citizen and voter. We also need to find a way forward to exercise the freedom to choose public representatives who are accountable and committed to protecting Mandela's legacy of forging a just democratic order. The biggest threat to that legacy is a culture that makes democracy a prisoner of special interest groups trading on the past. It would seem that Mandela's legacy is more likely to be undermined by those engaged in corrupt, nepotistic and unaccountable practices in both the public and private sectors, than by those who use their vote to punish unaccountability wherever it occurs. Is it not the role of citizens who want to protect that legacy to elect public representatives who can be trusted to be accountable in the promotion of the shared values and ideals of our democracy?

A critical question is the extent to which citizens are willing to exercise their freedom to make ethical choices. Why would voters continue to vote for a party they accuse of not delivering on its election promises, and then stage protests against the party during which they burn and destroy public property? Such destruction in the name of public protest violates the rights of others, including those of taxpayers who have to dig deeper into their pockets to fund the rebuilding of damaged public property. The same question applies to those in the private sector who make unethical decisions to collude in corrupt practices with politically connected people, and then blame corrupt politicians for demanding to be bribed to make enabling decisions for their businesses. The reality is that acquiescing to corrupt practices to advance one's business is both immoral and unethical. It is immoral in that it undermines the long-term good for business and society in general. It is unethical because the corruptor knows that it is wrong to perpetuate corruption by rewarding those involved. Corruption is a cancer that threatens the sustainability of businesses and societies.

———————

A related issue pertains to how we seem to have gravitated towards becoming a nation that has reduced 'being' into 'having', to borrow Fanon's words.[23] 'Being' is what defines us as human. We pride ourselves as South Africans on the value we place on *Ubuntu* – which could be translated as *beingness* – as a core of our philosophical orientation. One would have expected that 'being' would be a feature of our social relationships rather than 'having'. Unfortunately, for many the deprivations and injustices they suffered in the past as a result of social engineering that reduced the majority population to poverty have contributed to their obsession with material possessions. Many former political activists are compensating for lost time by focusing on the acquisition of wealth at all costs.

The coincidence of poverty with being discriminated against and disrespected as black people has created an understandable yearning to escape the trappings of poverty and marginality. The historical link between power and wealth for white people has predisposed the new elites to the obsession with 'having' as a symbol of power and worth. Ostentatious consumption in the form of expensive cars, clothes and houses have become key definitions of success. A significant proportion of South Africans have become caught up in the rat race to acquire more and more material resources in order to be seen to be wealthy and worthy as people.

While we need to celebrate the growth of middle and upper classes, especially the entry of young black professionals and business people – the so-called Black Diamonds[24] – we need to be mindful that we are not caught up in a culture in which 'having' is more important than 'being'. In 2005 Black Diamonds had R130 billion buying power out of a total of R300 billion for all black people. These figures rocketed to R180 billion and R335 billion respectively by 2007. The total buying power for

Conversations with My Sons and Daughters

white people was R230 billion in 2005 rising to R235 billion in 2007.[25] A more recent study by RamsayMedia Research Solutions in association with UCT Unilever Institute of Strategic Marketing shows that more than a third of the well-off in South Africa are black and the number is growing.[26] The greater participation of black people in the economy is paying dividends to those with access to opportunities: educated and trained people who are part of opportunity networks. For the rest, poverty and powerlessness continue.

South Africa has a Gini coefficient of 0.67, the highest in the world according to the latest World Bank Report.[27] What is even more alarming is that according to the National Development Plan released on 11 November 2011 the Gini coefficient has worsened to 0.7. The growing inequality in our society should remind us that our 'being' a society committed to social justice may be put at risk by the drive towards 'having'. The French philosopher Raymond Aron cautions us 'that too great a degree of inequality makes human community impossible'.[28]

We need to ask ourselves constantly whether our acquisition of wealth is interfering with building a society in which human community is valued. We have come to speak effortlessly of 'the poor' and 'the rich' as if people are defined by their material possessions or lack thereof. Poverty and wealth are becoming identity labels that divide our society into those one takes seriously or not, those one socialises with or not. The problem of 'us' and 'them' is exacerbated by apartheid's continuing geographic separation of those with access to opportunities derived from living near the facilities offered by cities, and poor people who continue to live in the ghettos. The most disturbing marker of this trend is how poor communities become invisible and inaudible as middle-class and wealthier people lock themselves behind higher and higher walls.

To add insult to injury, poor people have become props for politicians during election time when the latter pride themselves on visiting poor people in their homes and having their pictures taken in the deprived spaces that are home to so many. Without any hint of irony, some express shock at the extent of poverty and deprivation. With rhythmic regularity the shock and notes of concern fade with each passing election, only to be revived as a show for the next one. Only people who have been reduced to being subjects would tolerate such abusive relationships with those who are supposed to represent them; citizens would have the voice to say no to this cycle of abuse.

There is now solid evidence that gross inequality is not just morally wrong, but that it also undermines the well-being of all citizens. Through tracking studies in developed society, Richard Wilkinson and Kate Pickett show that

> ... if we are to gain further improvements in the real quality of life, we need to shift attention from material standards and economic growth to improving the psychological and social well-being of whole societies ... A proper understanding of what is going on could transform politics and the quality of life for all of us. It would change our experience of the world around us, change what we vote for, and change what we demand from politicians.[29]

The process of transition from the authoritarian, discriminatory and inequitable socio-economic and political system has not yet transformed our social relations to align them with the value system we adopted in our national constitution. We are at risk of growing cynicism towards the democratic values and human rights culture we espouse. Many young people have opted out of engagement with the political process because they are reluctant to be associated with the games that are played in the name of democracy. Some poke fun at these games, and this is reflected in the growing comedy genre in our public media. The satire of Pieter Dirk Uys (Evita Bezuidenhout) has inspired a new breed of young black South Africans to show politicians how ridiculous they are, but the majority remain completely disillusioned.

I am, however, encouraged to see a growing number of young people starting to explore ways in which they can become engaged citizens in order to pursue the dreams that defined the dawn of our democracy. Engaged citizens need to remind themselves that while all transitions are painful, the rewards of successful transformation make the journey worthwhile. We need to hold open conversations about the values we hold dear and how we are to resolve the conflicts of duty that inevitably arise in making ethical choices in a complex world. We cannot avoid the responsibility of exercising our rights to make choices as free citizens. There is no excuse for failure to apply one's mind to making those difficult choices. This is the responsibility of being human.

CHAPTER 4

HOW DO THE AGREED VALUES CASCADE INTO OUR GOVERNANCE PRACTICES?

Our national constitution stipulates clearly how our democracy is to be governed. It is to be a participatory democracy in which citizens are sovereign and are equal before the law. The Bill of Rights in Chapter 2 of the constitution sets out the workings of cooperative government at the local, provincial and national levels. There is no ambiguity about the commitment to a government that draws its legitimacy from transparent free and fair elections by all citizens eligible to vote. The society envisaged in our national constitution is one characterised by social justice, enabling all to develop their full potential to be productive citizens.

The systemic failure to establish and apply performance management systems in the public service reflects both a lack of political will and technical capacity to govern according to the precepts of our national constitution. We have failed to develop a system and a culture of accountability for living the dream of an inclusive democratic culture and vulnerable poor people are stunned by the extent to which they have been left behind in the post-1994 democratic process.

The question that stares us in the face is: Why have there been such systemic failures in aligning our system of governance and its performance with the values set out in our constitution? Are we simply another example of the inability of Africa's post-colonial governments to transcend the legacy of the past? My view is that we have fallen prey to two fatal flaws:

- We have fallen into the trap of heroic politics with the ANC governing as a liberation movement that has not transformed itself into a modern political party
- We have failed to tackle the challenges of systematic restructuring of the economy to lay the foundation for progressive realisation of socio-economic rights and inclusive prosperity

Unless we address these two fatal flaws, South Africa is likely to lurch from mediocre performance to social instability and worse. We are already witnessing some of the signs of decline.

Africa continues to wrestle with the transition from post-colonial underdevelopment to realise the dream of 'claiming the twenty-first century'.[30] For Africa to successfully claim its rightful place in the globally interconnected and interdependent world it will have to make a fundamental shift from liberation struggle politics to democratic politics. Africa suffers from weak political, social and economic institutional systems and frameworks for planning and implementing appropriate policies.

Systems of governance based on liberation movement politics have characterised many of the approaches of governments in post-colonial Africa and former leaders of resistance and liberation movements have tended to see themselves as the natural leaders of governments. No thought seems to have been given by African citizens and leaders to the possibility of a mismatch between the skills set required for governance and that of freedom fighters.

In *Architects of Poverty*[31] Moeletsi Mbeki identifies the failure of leadership by Africa's elites as being at the heart of its inability to harness its considerable natural and human resources to establish sustainable prosperity for its people. And at the heart of the failure of leadership is the lack of a frame of reference for governance that makes a fundamental break with the colonial past. Leaders of most liberation movements derived their education and training from the very systems they later set out to oppose or even wage war against. But opposition to a system does not necessarily signal a commitment to a radically different system of governance.

It is striking how many African countries have replicated the very colonial governance systems they purported to abhor. The very fact of Africa's countries today defining themselves as Francophone, Lusophone and Anglophone demonstrates how deeply Africa has imbibed the values, systems, languages and symbols – replete with white wigs – of their former masters. Embarrassing as this is, it is but an external manifestation of a deeper and more devastating reality which is that most former liberation movements have failed to make the transition into credible democratic governance machines.

Prince Mashele, in *The Death of Our Society*, puts the blame squarely on the failure to acknowledge 'the crippling trap that a number of post-colonial African societies have proven incapable of escaping heroism.'[32] Heroism is defined here as 'a way of thinking that makes multitudes of people believe that their social, political and economic fates depend on the actions or benevolence of special individuals in society who possess extraordinary abilities and powers that are beyond ordinary citizens.'[33] South Africa has not escaped this trap. As we shall discuss below, it seems that our country received the most complex and binding trap of them all. The blessing of a leader in the person of Nelson Rolihlahla Mandela as the hero of our struggle for liberation and the first president of democratic South Africa comes with the curse of entrapment. Our ability to escape the trap of heroic politics and make the transition to an open society and true multiparty democracy depends on our willingness to take the risk of going beyond liberation politics. Such a step requires vision and courage to forge a path that many African countries have failed to follow.

Let us focus on the following key issues:

- Leadership as the embodiment of dreams and ideals and the dilemmas of entitlement
- Mismatch between skills for governance of a modern democracy and those of the liberation struggle
- Clash of cultures between liberation and democratic governance politics

- Inadequate focus on sustainable development models in post-colonial Africa, including harnessing the opportunities of regional integration of Africa's economies to accelerate shared growth

Over time, leaders of liberation movements become the embodiment of the hopes, aspirations and determination of a people to make sacrifices for a future in which they can be a free people. The longer and the more vicious the struggle is, the more importance is attached to the leader to hold people together, inspire them and keep alive the hope that victory is certain even in the darkest moments.

Victors of wars of liberation in many former African colonies who have formed governments in the post-colonial period have had very poor track records. Even in Ghana, where no military or guerrilla war was fought, President Kwame Nkrumah was overwhelmed by the office of president of the first post-colonial country. His famous quotation 'seek ye first the political kingdom and all other things shall be added to you' proved difficult to translate into the realpolitik of post-colonial reconstruction and development. Opposition to colonialism had not necessarily prepared him for leadership in government, and taking over the reins of a state that was not yet transformed from its colonial foundations added to the challenges of governance.

Failure to undertake systematic transformation of the colonial economic base undermined opportunities for changing social relations to enable citizens to become active agents in the future of their country. Nkrumah faltered despite the support he had from his own people and neo-colonial intervention that had been expecting him to fail and watching him like a hawk circling its prey was quick to pounce. A coup supported by neo-colonial agents became inevitable and Ghana was to struggle for many decades under military governments before finding its way back to civilian politics.

Unfortunately, the strength of post-colonial leaders is no guarantee of success in governance. Take the Ugandan example of President Yoweri Museveni. Hailed as a hero after defeating dictators Idi Amin and Milton Obote, Museveni styled himself as a modern African leader who was determined not to become an obstacle to democratic elections and change in leadership. He inspired Uganda's people to slay the HIV/AIDS dragon which had a prevalence rate close to 18 per cent, forcing it down to around 8 per cent by campaigning for changes in the sexual practices and lifestyles that were driving the epidemic. Today, Museveni has entrenched himself as the only guarantor of democracy and progress in Uganda and he has denounced any civil society movement that poses a threat to his life presidency.

The same history has unfolded in Zimbabwe with President Robert Mugabe of the Zimbabwe African National Union (Zanu-PF). Mugabe evolved from a liberation struggle hero in 1975 to exemplary president of a thriving Zimbabwe in the 1980s, into the dictator of today. He has strangled his country's development and wrecked its future in order to entrench his leadership and the power base of his party. Zimbabwean citizens have become mere spectators in the political arena after years of giving Zanu-PF a blank cheque to govern, despite rising concerns about corruption, nepotism and misguided economic policies. By the time they opted to support a trade union inspired party, The Movement for Democratic Change (MDC), the decline had gone too far.

The sense of entitlement to govern was exemplified by the military stating boldly that they were not willing to salute anyone but Mugabe.

Zimbabwean citizens who were misguided enough to vote for the MDC were physically assaulted and many were killed. The majority of professionals and business people are living in exile in our country and elsewhere in the world and Zimbabwe is a shell of its former self.

South Africa was blessed with a hero of the struggle, President Nelson Mandela, who showed wisdom and generosity by his willingness to forge a new pathway in the face of a stalemate in the struggle for freedom between those who opposed apartheid and those who supported it. His heroic actions went further in settling for a process of reconciliation, rather than retribution, that sought to move the country forward as a united nation. In addition, he set a fine example by not clinging to power as the inaugural president but stepping aside for the younger generation to take the country into the twenty-first century.

President Mandela's exemplary leadership has unfortunately not freed us from the 'trap of heroic politics'. If anything, his towering leadership has exacerbated the problem by making the link between Mandela the person, the ANC as a liberation-movement-turned-governing-party, the government and the state emotionally tight. Succession struggles within the ANC have become a regular feature of our political life since the 1990s. Instead of focusing on who would be the best leader for each stage of our transition, the concern is to find who is in line to take control of the leadership of the ANC, the government and the state in order to advance the priorities of their circle of supporters. The ordinary citizen features nowhere on the various agendas being pursued.

The Thabo Mbeki/Cyril Ramaphosa battle for the deputy presidency and the subsequent conspiracy allegations against Tokyo Sexwale, Cyril Ramaphosa and Mathews Phosa in the run-up to the 2004 elections, set the scene for a competition for power. The three were accused by President Thabo Mbeki's government of plotting to oust him as president of the ANC and of the republic. Ironically, the assertion that it is the ANC's tradition that one does not put oneself forward as a contestant for leadership but waits to be deployed or anointed flies in the face of the brutal and fierce battles for power that have taken place. The most visible and brutal fight culminated in the election in 2007 of Jacob Zuma as president of the ANC and the recall of Thabo Mbeki as president of the republic. The battle for control of state power reached new heights and the upcoming elective conference in Mangaung in December 2012 is throwing up more intrigues as individuals position themselves behind various contenders.

The tragic outcome of these struggles for power has been the undermining of good governance and of the process of strengthening democracy. In the first instance, the enormous energy devoted to shadow boxing by political leaders and public servants at local, provincial and national levels detracts from the responsibilities of governance. Frequent changes in these political structures have had a serious impact on the continuity and effectiveness of the governance process. In Gauteng Province, Premier Nomvula Mokonyane had no sooner settled into her position in 2009 than her competitors started agitating for her removal as Chair of the ANC in Gauteng. They succeeded months later and installed Paul Mashatile, her predecessor, as Chair and her effective political boss. She can hardly move without being second guessed and her attempts to undo questionable schemes formulated under her predecessor and to hold accountable those responsible for them have been curtailed. The same situation applies at most local levels where those deployed to public service jobs are subject to political leaders in the local authority who can clip their wings at will.

Competition for power has had a major impact on state institutions. The anti-Mbeki campaigners prior to the 2007 ANC conference in Polokwane complained about his abuse of state institutions, asserting that the intelligence system, the police, the National Prosecuting Authority (NPA), and the Directorate of Special Operations (the Scorpions) were being used to fight political battles against his competitors. The more than 700 corruption charges against Jacob Zuma and his dismissal as deputy president of the republic were cited as evidence of the abuse of state institutions. The charges against Zuma were dropped in early 2009, paving the way for him to become president of the republic. Ironically, the basis for the dismissal was said to be intercepted communication between supporters of Thabo Mbeki and NPA officials furnished to Zuma's lawyers by national intelligence operatives.

In a further ironic twist, Jacob Zuma, as president of the republic, is being accused by his detractors within the ANC of abusing state institutions to silence his political competitors and critics. Succession battles for leadership of the ANC are raging ahead of the 2012 Mangaung elective conference and the democratic governance system is being further undermined by the power struggles within the ANC. The pretence that ANC leaders do not compete for power is the root cause of these battles but there seems to be no awareness of the cynicism that this is generating amongst both young and old voters. The pretence persists as a fig-leaf to hide behind in the naked pursuit of power under the guise of service by 'heroes of the struggle'.

A more worrying matter for our conversations is that this pretence, which is eroding the idealism of our constitutional democracy, is tolerated by citizens and by voters in particular. Why are the owners of South Africa's commonwealth not calling those entrusted with public office to order and demanding that they focus on the task of transforming our society and establishing a more just social system? This question is an urgent one for you as my sons and daughters whose future is being put at risk by these continuing intrigues.

––––––––––

There is a sense of entitlement in the assertion that those who sacrificed their youth to the armed struggle have a right to lead and govern. This sense of entitlement introduces a real dilemma in that those who fought hard for freedom and who feel strongly that they should enjoy the spoils of being in government do not necessarily have the capacity to govern. The right to govern a modern, sophisticated socio-economic and political system has to be balanced with the right of citizens to be governed competently. Most freedom fighters lack the most basic skills needed for good governance. Their military training as guerrilla fighters has not necessarily prepared them for the value-based approach to governance which is central to our constitutional democracy.

The transformation of the state from one that served a minority government into one that serves the majority is a task that has yet to be achieved. The focus thus far has been on taking control of the state, rather than on transforming it into a platform for democratic governance. This should come as no surprise at all because South Africa is no exception to other post-colonial experiences. The driving force of freedom fighters was opposition to the injustices committed by the discriminatory colonial conquerors who ruled them and little space was devoted to defining and discussing alternative systems.

Alternatives such as the Unity Movement's Ten Point Programme, the

ANC's Freedom Charter and the PAC's 'Africa for Africans' that were defined during the struggle were sketchy and the realities they painted had been overtaken by the shifting political and economic realities by the time freedom came. The negotiated settlement that ushered in democracy in 1994 and the adoption of the national constitution in 1996 do not seem to have laid a strong enough foundation for good government. Increasing public rhetoric about returning to the Freedom Charter as the supreme guiding document for economic policy reflects the failure of the new dispensation to anchor economic governance within the framework and values of the national constitution. Harking back to the Freedom Charter, a 1955 document adopted by a sector of the population of the time, is a political game that has less to do with the ideals of that document than with positioning a segment of the ANC in the leadership struggle for the 2012 elective conference.

Even if one were to accept post-liberation frameworks such as the Freedom Charter, one has to acknowledge that they suffered from inadequate space for internal debates to spell out the details and alternative policy options that were being proposed. At the time security concerns as well as lack of skills curtailed the level of open participation by ordinary members of liberation movements. Much of what passes as the people's documents was drafted by a few people in the elite leadership of the liberation movement. This much was admitted to by Ben Turok in the case of the Freedom Charter.[34] It is one thing to pronounce on what is to be, but totally another for a society to understand the implications of policy options put to it. Moreover, specific instances such as nationalisation as understood in the mid-1950s raise a totally different set of policy challenges in the twenty-first century.

An even bigger challenge in acknowledging the inadequacy of skills to govern in post-apartheid South Africa is the historical racist notion of associating black people with lack of knowledge and skill. This association was used to justify exclusion of black people from representation and governance of their countries during the colonial period. The operating principle of colonial governments was to install 'civilised government' over barbaric people. Even so-called progressive liberal political parties in the late colonial period bought into the notion of a qualified franchise that set educational and other criteria for acceptance as a citizen with the right to vote.

The cruel irony of the inequity of excluding people from exercising their democratic rights on grounds of lack of educational and social standing was lost on many colonialists. How could they justify the fairness of a qualified franchise whilst denying the majority population access to education? The consequence of this inequity is that it provides a moral argument for dismissing meritocracy as a basis for post-colonial public service. It also provides the political cover for those in government not acknowledging lack of skills and knowledge, for this would be buying into the notion that black people are not ready to govern.

Tragically, even in those cases where liberation movements sent their people for training in anticipation of the requirements for governing modern systems, many of those skilled people were not necessarily utilised in the post-colonial period. Of those who were utilised, few survived beyond the heady days after Uhuru. The stresses and strains of running a democracy soon overpowered the idealism of comradeship. Senior political leaders seldom manage to put their personal insecurities aside in favour of using the best available talents and skills to meet the needs of society. Many talented public servants became marginalised and some were literally hounded out of jobs because they disagreed with their former comrades on what was technically appropriate for sustainable development.

Another major challenge for liberation movements has been how to make the transition from liberators to governing political parties. The skills set required of liberation movement leaders is in material respects different from that required for governance in complex modern socio-economic and political systems. Many of those who were at the forefront of the freedom struggle were often uneducated and were led by a very small band of educated elite. Liberation movement leaders, especially those engaged in waging wars against their oppressors, had a style of leadership appropriate for the task at hand. Authoritarianism is functional in a militaristic institutional environment, but not in a democratic one and the technical skills essential for governance and managing modern socio-economic systems in a democratic polity were not a focus of liberation movements.

Governing a modern polity and economy has never been as complex as it is today in our interdependent and interconnected competitive world. When we made the change in our polity in 1994 South Africa had a head start in inheriting a sophisticated economy and the basic infrastructure needed to drive economic growth. We were also blessed with a government that understood the importance of transforming the macro-economic system we inherited that had served the privileged minority but was inappropriate as a platform for a modern open economy.

Much of the early success was attributable to the skilled people who were both retained from the past and recruited to champion and restructure our macro-economy. The same focus on skills has stood our

Revenue Service in good stead and turned it into one the most efficient, progressive, and transparent tax systems in the world. Other areas of governance in the first post-apartheid administration such as Water and Forestry under the late Kader Asmal, Justice and the Judiciary System under the late Abdullah Omar, and Agriculture and Land Affairs under Derek Hanekom, were also headed by competent people who were able to set the frameworks for good governance on sound scientific foundations.

But the success of the economic sectors has not translated into prosperity on the ground for the majority. A major weakness in all post-apartheid administrations has been in translating excellent macro-level policies into effective implementable programmes. For example, macro-economic stability has not been accompanied by effective micro-economic interventions to promote entrepreneurship through small and medium enterprises that hold the greatest promise of employment and livelihoods. We have witnessed jobless growth in our post-apartheid environment whilst unemployment has grown to alarming proportions, especially amongst young people. What is missing is a transformative economic policy framework driven by a competent public service.

———————

Transference of liberation movement institutional cultures into a democracy creates serious problems of a clash of cultures. Organisational cultures of liberation movements differ in important respects from those of political parties operating in a democracy. The differences relate not only to internal workings of the political machineries, but spill over into relationships between these political machineries and actors in the external environment, including the citizens of a democracy. Attitudes to the state by liberation movement parties also create significant constitutional and other governance crises.

The dominant institutional cultural traits that make liberation movements succeed in waging struggles for freedom are often the ones that contribute to their failures as governing parties. A few examples are listed here and will be discussed in some detail below:

- A 'them' and 'us' approach versus promoting national unity;
- respect for political competition versus hegemony;
- meritocracy versus set-asides for loyalists;
- equality before the law versus protection of comrades;
- open debates versus following the party line;
- tolerance of differences versus unity at all costs, and so on.

We need to try to understand why it is difficult to transcend the clash of cultures between the politics of liberation movements and those essential to modern democracies.

The passion that fuels liberation struggles is based on a deep sense of injustice against one's group by another. 'Them' and 'us' becomes the dividing line between those for and those against one's struggle for freedom and justice. The fervour that keeps the energy flowing in the struggle is the sense of righteousness of one's cause in contrast to the inequity of the enemy and over time it becomes second nature that those who are not for us are against us. Elite packs that often precede transitions to democracy rarely touch on the healing process needed to bind former enemies into fellow citizens. On the contrary, many leaders of liberation movements strategically agree to settlement terms that are suboptimal only to later fan the embers of anger in their support base to ensure retention of loyalty to the governing party regardless of its performance. They actively cultivate their indispensability as the protectors of ordinary citizens against the resurgence of the former enemy who could steal their freedom and return them to bondage. Such leaders present themselves to citizens as insurance policies against regression to the oppressive past.

Mistrust of anyone who was not part of the liberation movement as defined by protagonists of the 'them' and 'us' approach is actively promoted by some leaders to enhance their appeal as the only legitimate political representatives of poor people. Those holding alternative views on political and policy options are labelled as counter-revolutionaries. The emotive content of the counter-revolutionary label is deliberately intended to silence dissent on pain of being marginalised as a threat to the gains made by those who fought for radical political change. Even our highly regarded judicial system and its judges are not spared the counter-revolutionary label. Judgements that challenged the ANC's approach to issues of public interest pertaining to Jacob Zuma's corruption charges in the run-up to his appointment as president of South Africa were regarded as a sign of anti-revolutionary action.

President Robert Mugabe of Zimbabwe has perfected the art of 'us' and 'them'. A country that showed immense promise is being ruined by rampant corruption and undermining of the rule of law. The resuscitation of Britain as a colonial master that is threatening Zimbabwean sovereignty is played out with such fervour that it would be amusing if it were not so tragic. Any Zimbabwean who objects to the brutal land invasions is labelled a supporter of the recolonisation of Zimbabwe. Mugabe even created a ruthless rag-tag army of young desperadoes calling them 'military veterans' of the liberation army to lead the attacks on farmers and farm workers. Many of these 'military veterans' had not been born when the liberation war ended. The Zimbabwean 'military veteran' phenomenon is an indication of how much currency is attached to the entitlement of those who fought for freedom to make decisions regardless of their impact on the rest of the citizens. It also gives such veterans the right to bestow the title to segments of the population of their choosing. It is an omnipotence that is incompatible with the idea of freedom in a democracy.

The Movement for Democratic Change (MDC), born out of the frustrations of the trade union movement and ordinary citizens with the increasing repression of critical voices, has been demonised as puppets of the West. The popular appeal of the MDC led to electoral successes in 2000, when it won 57 out of 61 seats in the national parliament despite the intimidation and harassment of its supporters. Again, in 2002 Morgan Tsvangirai won the presidential election which was stolen with the connivance of the South African government. The 2005 parliamentary elections were clearly won by the MDC as monitored on electronic media, but Zanu-PF simply refused to relinquish the reins of power.

The ambivalence of many African leaders towards democracy has enabled Robert Mugabe to hang on to power. South Africa's President Mbeki's controversial role in negotiating a compromise deal that simply reinstalled Robert Mugabe as president with Morgan Tsvangirai as prime minister reflects an ambivalence towards respecting the will of the voters in an election. South Africa, as broker of the deal, has not enforced the provisions that could have laid the foundation for free and fair elections after a cooling-off period. Zimbabwe remains a violator of human rights with little indication of the emergence of a less repressive dispensation.

The compromise deal brokered by President Mbeki remains a troubling example of how African leaders continue to break the promise of good governance they made to themselves and their fellow citizens in adopting the New Partnership for Africa's Development (NEPAD) in July 2001 in Lusaka, Zambia. Robert Mugabe was rewarded with continuing as president for his refusal to accept electoral defeat. He treats the real winner of the presidency, Morgan Tsvangirai, who is prime minister, with utter contempt. African leaders in the Southern African Development Community (SADC) and the rest of the African Union have failed to show resolve in holding Robert Mugabe to the letter of the compromise agreement reached to hold Zimbabwe together. One cannot help but conclude that the political will to hold peers accountable to democratic principles is trumped by the solidarity of former comrades in arms to be loyal to one another as leaders in post-colonial Africa.

The issue of loyalty in liberation movements beyond the struggle period flows from these kinds of sentiments. Loyalty is a premium requirement in the struggle for freedom, given the risks of infiltration by enemy agents, and letting down one's guard and becoming open to other influences might be suicidal not just for the individual but for the whole movement. In many cases turncoats led to tragedies where whole groups of fighters were wiped out and these traumatic experiences left very deep trust deficits in those who had to live with the realities of betrayal. Political settlement talks intended to enable the bridging of the trust gulf between the parties rarely succeed in doing so beyond the symbolic ritual handshakes. It is rare to have active processes of reconciliation between former warring factions that will enable them to forge a common future.

You, as the leaders of the future, need to be concerned about the rise in the rhetoric in our politics that echoes the language of retribution that the Truth and Reconciliation Commission sought to banish. The games that political actors play to position themselves for power and patronage are dangerous games that must be resisted before they engulf us in an inferno of hatred and conflict.

Identity politics, understood as the mobilisation of identity consciousness in order to create a mass base of support for the ruling classes and the elite generally, assumes highly contentious tones in South Africa. Given the legacy of apartheid and its inequity, there is a pseudo-moral basis for keeping the 'them' and 'us' divisions alive in the name of securing the gains of the anti-apartheid struggle. It is alarming to see how identity politics is being deployed to secure their support bases by the likes of leaders of the ANC Youth League, Julius Malema, the President of the Black Management Forum and Government Spokesman, Jimmy Manyi, and others within the ruling party.

Africa has had to deal with the tragic consequences of identity politics before and we need to learn from this before it is too late. Nigeria's post-colonial government – the First Republic (October 1960-January 1966) collapsed into a civil war due to the inherited 'invented traditions' that sowed divisions between 'them' and 'us' such as Northerner versus Southerner; Muslim versus Christian; Hausa-Fulani versus Yoruba; etc.[35] The high cost Nigeria paid during the civil war undermined its development, delaying its transition into a prosperous democracy by many decades. The current government led by President Goodluck Jonathan has the opportunity of demonstrating that Nigeria has the political will to consolidate democracy without resorting to identity politics.

The danger of identity politics lies in its criminalisation of a sector of the population by virtue of some ascribed criterion and such criminalisation becomes even more dangerous if it coincides and resonates with historic injustices. The Rwandan genocide is a case in point. The divide and conquer colonial policies of the Belgians laid the foundations for a system in which the minority Tutsis (15 per cent), favoured for their appearance – tall, sharp noses and lighter skin – dominated government. The majority Hutus with darker skin, flatter noses and shorter stature were treated as inferior. Tensions that had persisted since the 1962 independence war that overthrew the Tutsi monarchy fuelled the civil war which started in 1990 pitting the Hutu government against the Rwanda Patriotic Front (largely Tutsi exiles) and exploded into the 1993 killing of two thousand Tutsis. Attempts to reconcile the warring factions failed because President Juvenal Habyarimana was unwilling to include the Tutsi minority in government.

This was the powder keg that needed only a small spark to ignite it into the catastrophe it became in 1994. The shooting down of President Habyarimana's plane on 6 April 1994 unleashed a savagery that led to the slaughter of nearly a million people, the majority of whom were Tutsis, although Hutus who refused to kill their Tutsi neighbours also perished. It is poignant that this genocide coincided with our own transition to democracy in April 1994. Rwanda has been bold in acknowledging this most painful and shameful event in its history by building a graphic Genocide Monument in Kigali. The skulls, identity documents and other personal effects serve to remind visitors that these are the remains of ordinary women, men and children whose only crime was to belong to the wrong group or to socialise with and protect those whom they were ordered to kill. Rwanda's people are still working to heal the wounds left by this tragedy, painfully conscious of how easy it is for a small spark to reignite the inferno that engulfed their country in 1994.

The gay abandon with which the ANC allows its members to criminalise people because of the colour of their skin is a matter of grave concern for our young and fragile democracy. Playing on the raw sentiments of the failure of the post-apartheid socio-economic redress measures and the emotive land reform process are threats to social stability and instead of confronting the causes of the failure so that agreed policies can be effectively implemented, racism is being used as the scapegoat. For example, on the advice of the World Bank, the South African government set the target of transferring 30 per cent of agricultural land within the first five years after the 1994 elections by means of the so-called 'willing buyer, willing seller' approach. By 1999 only 1 per cent of that target had been achieved. By 2008/09, nearly ten years after the original deadline, only 11.1 per cent of that original target figure had been transferred.[36] On the other hand, the land restitution processes have proceeded significantly better. Of the 79 696 valid claims, 4 296 were still outstanding by 2009. In other words, 94.6 per cent of the claims had been settled.[37]

Despite acknowledgement by Gugile Kwinti, Minister of Rural Development and Land Reform, of the government's contribution to the failures so far, emotions of poor people are still being stirred by other ANC leaders for power political purposes. The silence of ANC president Jacob Zuma in the face of provocative statements adds weight to the danger. Take ANC Youth League President Julius Malema's statement in Kimberley in April 2011 in the silent presence of President Jacob Zuma:

> White people should be treated as criminals for 'stealing' land
> from black people. They (whites) have turned our land into game

farms … The 'willing buyer/willing seller' (system) has failed. We must take the land without paying. Once we agree they have stolen the land, we can agree they are criminals and they must be treated as such.[38]

The potency of the call to ascribe criminality to white people lies in linking it to the emotive land question. The failure of the 'willing buyer/willing seller' system is touted without examination as the basis for declaring white people as criminals. This approach has frightening similarities with Robert Mugabe's approach in Zimbabwe; he has yet to acknowledge the role of corruption and cronyism in the stalled land reforms in the late 1990s. The most chilling phrase in Malema's statement is: 'Once we agree they have stolen the land, we can agree they are criminals and they must be treated as such.' Who are 'we' and who are 'they'? By what mechanism is the agreement to be reached that 'they' are criminals? Are all white farm owners criminals who have stolen the land and thus must be 'treated as such'?

The ANC is at risk of allowing itself to be used as an instrument to undo the hard work of forging reconciliation in our society and thus undermining President Mandela's legacy. The reconciliation efforts of so many people in all walks of life over the last two decades, including the Truth and Reconciliation Commission (TRC), ongoing civil society groups and many individual efforts (including those of farm owners), must not be sabotaged by such reckless utterances. The moving musical play *Rewind*, conceived and composed by Philip Miller and launched at the Baxter Theatre in May 2011, forces us to remember just how painful our journey from our divided brutal past has been. The play reminds us, in song and dance, of how many people emptied themselves in TRC testimonies to build the bridge to the future so that Mandela's democracy could become stable and equitable. Why do we allow anyone to put our future at risk through reckless statements? We rely on you, as Malema's age group, to stand up and be counted as not sharing his views, otherwise your silence will come back to haunt you.

———————

It follows from the above analysis that legitimacy of political competition is not part of the DNA of most liberation movements. There is often a sense of entitlement on the part of freedom fighters of the dominant movement to the support of the citizens of a democracy as a reward for the sacrifices they made during the struggle for freedom. The contributions of other liberation movements, let alone those of citizens as individuals and groups, are often devalued or air-brushed from history. Effective use of rumour, innuendo, and worse, is employed to silence competitors for power who are keenly watched, both inside and outside the dominant movement, to prevent their ascent to power.

Zimbabwe is a tragic and dramatic illustration of how vested interests in sustaining the legitimacy and dominance of liberation leadership have held the country captive and destroyed its potential for greatness. Not only has Zanu-PF under Robert Mugabe reversed the gains Zimbabwe made after its liberation in 1980 by plundering its economy, but it has turned on its own people and murdered them in cold blood. Former guerrillas were turned into militia trained by North Koreans to eliminate the Zimbabwe African People's Union (Zapu) as a competitor for political power and countless women and men were shot mercilessly in Matebeleland to establish Zanu-PF's hegemony. But the carnage did not end there. The failure in the 1980-1990s to implement the land reform process agreed under the Lancaster House Agreement, resulted in part from the greed of Zanu-PF oligarchs to enrich themselves. It was this greed that turned Zimbabwe from a bread basket into a basket case.

The 2011 Ibrahim Index of Good Governance[39] shows a growing divergence between improvements in Sustainable Economic Opportunity and Participation and Human Rights in Africa's 53 countries. For example, North African countries such as Egypt, Libya and Tunisia ranked 2, 12 and 5 respectively on Sustainable Economic Opportunity, while on Participation and Human Rights they ranked 39, 51 and 42 respectively. The imbalance between economic and political governance and respect for human rights partly explains the civic conflict from late 2010 to 2011 that led to the fall of the regimes that had dominated these countries for decades. These struggles were led by young people who felt excluded from participation in the polity and economic opportunities in their own countries and they achieved what many believed unthinkable.

How is South Africa faring on this score? South Africa's Ibrahim Index, ranking at 5 overall behind Mauritius, Cape Verde, Seychelles and Botswana, is a mediocre performance given its position as the largest economy in Africa and a society that had a laudable start to its democracy in 1994. There are disturbing signs of decline in the rankings on key areas of governance between 2006 and 2010. The Sustainable Economic Opportunity ranking has fallen from 5 to 7, whilst Participation and Human Rights ranking has also declined from 1 to 5. The Personal Safety sub-category ranking places South Africa in the league of war-torn countries at 44 out of 53. The lack of personal safety reflects the rampant crime that has engulfed our society, fuelled in part by growing inequalities and ineffectual crime prevention and policing.

There is no doubt that ours has been a complicated transition to democracy. Our liberation struggle was the longest in Africa and it meandered through difficult periods. The armed struggle, by the admission of its protagonists, was not the roaring success that is often claimed.[40] The liberation movement was not only fragmented in exile within and between different organisations, but its external and internal wings were also fractured. In the end these fragments were glued together by the force of personality of Nelson Mandela who led the political negotiations that ended in a settlement between freedom fighters and the apartheid government. But the glue has not held. The ANC continues to be shaken by internal power struggles beyond the Polokwane palace coup that unseated Thabo Mbeki in 2007 as leader of the ANC and in 2008 as president of South Africa.

The Thabo Mbeki presidency embedded the culture of non-account-ability of the ruling party to the citizens of South Africa. He seemed to believe in the values of central control and command rather than those of the participatory governance that was envisaged for our democracy. Opposition parties were regarded as threats to democracy rather than the essential pillars of a multiparty democracy. President Mbeki showed little respect for leaders of opposition parties or, indeed, for parliament which he seldom attended other than to address the Assembly at its opening or on other important occasions such as the presentation of the Budget Speech. He dealt with parliament largely through his Representative or Liaison Officer, Smuts Ngonyama, and appearances to answer questions from members of parliament were a rarity.

President Mbeki seemed to be allergic to non-governmental organisations and other organs of civil society. He seems to have taken the view that since the government had been elected by the majority of voters it was entitled to govern without interference from opposition parties or civil society organisations. This hostility soon permeated the culture of the public service. The irony that many public servants were civil society activists appears to have been lost on them, or has it? Could it be that civil society groups were also seen as a threat to central control and command?

President Thabo Mbeki had another fatal flaw. He firmly believed that he was *the* person – possibly the *only* person – who could chart the path to a successful transition to democracy and reposition South Africa and Africa in general as serious players in global politics. His biographer Mark Gevisser had this to say of Thabo Mbeki's interpretation of his mandate when he came to power:

> … his mandate was nothing less than the salvation of his people. Mbeki had said repeatedly, in one way or another, that he was haunted by the nightmare of a seething majority that would boil over into rebellion because its dream of liberation had been deferred rather than redeemed.[41]

Thabo Mbeki's presidency was framed by this mandate; nothing else mattered. The 'saviour mandate' would weigh heavily on the shoulders of anyone carrying such a mantle, but it would also empower the mandated person to remove or ignore any obstacle placed in the way of discharging his responsibilities. Tolerance of other viewpoints would threaten the clarity of vision which inspired the leader and infuse his policy and governance stances. It was no surprise that President Mbeki was so assured of his own intellectual and other capabilities that he did not even entertain the possibility that he might be wrong on some key issues.

The most devastating policy position he took was with respect to HIV/AIDS. Not only was this a new pandemic which no one else was

Conversations with My Sons and Daughters

confident enough to pronounce on with any certainty, but in HIV one was confronting a highly agile virus that was capable of embedding itself in the human body through rapid mutation and adaptation to new ecosystems. President Mbeki, however, opted for the views of a minority of discredited scientists who denied the evidence of a link between HIV and AIDS. This minority view ignored the core values of the scientific method which permits one to challenge conventional views with proven reproducible alternative ones. Even more disturbing was that President Mbeki ignored local scientists and demonised anyone who held alternative views to his own, including scientists such as Professor Malegapuru Makgoba, who was then head of the Medical Research Council (MRC) of South Africa. President Mbeki's stance was so demotivating for scientists that many abandoned high level scientific positions or left the country. Professor Makgoba, for example, left the MRC to become vice chancellor of the University of KwaZulu-Natal.

President Thabo Mbeki was at pains to explain to all who would listen that the supposed link between HIV and AIDS was part of a conspiracy between scientists and the pharmaceutical industry to sell antiretrovirals to hapless Africans in order to keep Africa impoverished.[42] He also saw the link as an assault on African masculinity by white racists and said as much in his 12 October 2001 Z K Matthews Lecture at the University of Fort Hare.[43] His insistence on holding such a contrarian view was likened by Helen Epstein to Coriolanus in Shakespeare's tragedy and quoted by Gevisser: 'Like Coriolanus, Mbeki has stubbornly decided to debate AIDS on his own terms ... by denying 15 years of research on HIV/AIDS. As he does so, his pride may well destroy his own people.'[44]

South Africa is now wrestling with the resultant challenge of dealing with the negative impact of HIV/AIDS on its human and social capital base. Destruction wrought by President Mbeki's denialism continues to take its toll on our young democracy. In 2009, 5.6 million or 11 per cent of the population were living with HIV/AIDS, and 17.8 per cent of those in the 15 to 49 year age group were affected. Amongst women in the 25 to 29 year age group 30 per cent were living with the virus, whilst 25 per cent of men in the 30 to 34 year age group were similarly affected. Close to two million children have lost one or both parents to HIV/AIDS. These figures capture only the tip of the iceberg of the devastation that has befallen South Africa as a result of failure of leadership by successive governments since the 1982 diagnosis of HIV in two male flight attendants.

Statistics South Africa was also affected by the denial of the link between the increasing deaths in the general population and frightening escalations of maternal, infant and child mortality rates. Death certificates became instruments of denial. Causes of death from HIV/AIDS related illnesses were distorted to ridiculous levels prompting cartoonists to depict emaciated corpses with 'toothache' as the cause of death. The World Health Organisation (WHO) corrected misclassified HIV/AIDS deaths between 1996 and 2006 showing a rise in mortality from 19 to 48 per cent in 2006. The researchers concluded that between 1996 and 2006 about 94 per cent of deaths from HIV/AIDS were misclassified.[45]

The deployment approaches adopted under President Mbeki were most damaging, driven only by his desire to surround himself with staunch loyalists who could be entrusted with discharging his mandate. He seems to have focused his attention on the Economic Cluster where competent people were the norm in contrast to the Social Sector Cluster where competence was the exception. Able and competent people within the ANC who could have made remarkable contributions to the development of our democracy were often not given the opportunity to compete for available positions. Instead, incompetent people were deployed simply because they had political clout or were blindly loyal to the leader, which inevitably resulted in an undermining of the government's capacity to govern.

A notable case in this regard was the late Dr Manto Tshabalala-Msimang, who was appointed Minister of Heath in 1999 despite her poor track record as a health professional. Convicted in 1976 for stealing valuables from patients when she worked as a medical doctor in a Botswana hospital, Dr Manto Tshabalala-Msimang will go down in history as the disgraceful face of South Africa's HIV/AIDS denialism. Her embarrassing performance at the 2006 World AIDS Conference in Toronto demonstrated the extent to which she had descended into absurdity. The South Africa Exhibition Poster focused on her pet subjects: beetroot, ubejane (a herbal mixture) and everything but antiretrovirals. Dr Tshabalala-Msimang exemplified the dangers of blind loyalty to a political leader.

Disregard for competence resulted in the destruction of the health system in the name of transformation. A recent Development Bank of Southern Africa (DBSA) Review[46] details the severe skills mismatch in the management incumbents at provincial, district and larger complex hospitals. Teachers, nurses and others with low level skills have been appointed to run complex systems they are not in the least familiar with. The deterioration of the health system from the primary, secondary and tertiary levels leaves one shell-shocked that a country with a high level of sophistication in health science capabilities could descend this low. It is a painful demonstration of the cost of deployment strategies of a liberation movement party that has failed to make the transition to a governance party.

Parliament as an instrument for public accountability was neutralised and rendered nothing more than a rubber stamp under President Mbeki's leadership. Our national constitution elaborates on the principle of separation of powers under which parliament has to hold the executive accountable for performance on policies and against budgets legislated by parliament. The deployment policies referred to above, combined with the list system under our proportional representation electoral system, give the president of the ANC as the governing party power over the MPs who are supposed to hold him and his cabinet accountable. How can MPs be expected to stand up for what is right if that will put their jobs on the line? MPs' salaries are quite substantial at approximately R800 000 per annum and putting such a high reward at risk for most members of parliament who, but for their deployment, might otherwise have been unemployed, is not a reasonable expectation.

A culture of accountability cannot develop and flourish under such a system. A case in point here were the appointments to the board of the SABC towards the end of President Mbeki's tenure. His Parliamentary Representative, Smuts Ngonyama, literally instructed MPs to agree to a proposed list which was desired by the presidency rather than follow the transparent interview, ranking and recommendation process that is procedurally correct.[47]

State institutions supporting constitutional democracy as detailed in Chapter 9 of the constitution, such as the Public Protector, Human Rights Commission and National Prosecuting Authority, were also undermined by political interference. They became less and less independent and offered little critique of the executive authority. The boundaries between state, government, the party, and the president have over the years become more and more blurred and power became increasingly centralised during the Mbeki presidency. Performance management within the public sector progressively reflected the value of proximity to power rather than effort.

In 2006 President Mbeki asked parliament to appoint an ad hoc committee to review Chapter 9 and its associated institutions. The committee, chaired by the late Kader Asmal, released its report in 2007. Its findings identified major weaknesses, significant administrative and other legal gaps as well as duplication and lack of coherence that undermined the mandates and efficiencies of the institutions. The 16 recommendations of the Report remain just that.[48] The Report is languishing with many others because of the lack of political will to address problems identified in them. Almost the perfect silencer of evidence-based policy making – let the experts speak, then ignore them!

Despite setting up independent commissions to examine some of the weaknesses we have mentioned, President Mbeki consistently ignored their reports. The Van Zyl Slabbert Commission on the Electoral System is just one example. Van Zyl Slabbert was a loyal and passionate South African who dedicated himself to breaking the impasse between traditional white politics and the aspirations of the majority black population. He resigned from his position as leader of the Progressive Federal Party in 1986 after seven years at the helm and established the Institute for a Democratic South Africa (IDASA) to broker talks about a political settlement between the apartheid government and liberation movements led by the ANC. Among his Commission's recommendations was the need for an electoral system that addresses both direct constituency and proportional representation in our parliamentary system, which could be summed up as a single member constituency balanced by a national closed party list.[49] The core principles that guided the Commission were aligned to those of the constitution: fairness, inclusiveness, simplicity and accountability. Voters need to have a direct say in who represents their interests and be able to hold that person accountable. In addition, we need a system that reduces the risk of 'winner takes all' which could deny significant minority citizens the right to have their voices heard in parliament.

Right now, the issue of lack of accountability is a major contributor to the weakness of our democracy. Many of you as voters feel discouraged from exercising your duty to vote, frustrated because of the little impact you feel you can have on the system of governance. The futility of voting for a party that then used the vote to appoint people whom voters had rejected as local representatives came alive vividly during the May 2011 municipal elections. Communities expressed their views clearly yet they were ignored, resulting in unnecessary conflict and public violence. The report of the Van Zyl Slabbert Commission contains recommendations that could address these weaknesses in our systems, but it is gathering dust somewhere in the corridors of power.

The Zuma presidency has already shown even more worrying evidence of continuing the approach to governance as a right of the ANC rather than as a responsibility to citizens. His path to the presidency was the most blatant statement by the ANC of the extent to which it is prepared to disregard the most fundamental values of our national constitution to achieve its purposes. Every rule was broken to make sure that Jacob Zuma did not face his day in court to answer serious allegations of corruption that had sent his business partner and sponsor, Shabir Shaik, to jail. No stone was left unturned to prevent Zuma's court appearance, despite his earlier statements (before the December 2007 ANC meeting in Polokwane) that he wanted to clear his name in court. As we have already noted, privileged state intelligence information not available to any private citizen was made available to his lawyers to prepare his defence and to scuttle the charges on the grounds that his prosecution was politically motivated. The nub of the issue was that ANC internal succession conflicts had spilled over into the legal and judicial system and undermined the rule of law.

The capture of state institutions by the ANC made access to this information possible. The principle of equality before the law was trampled upon. Settling internal conflicts within the governing party came at the expense of important principles of our constitution, but the irony of the president's role as guardian of the country's constitution appears to have been lost on the ANC. The president's oath of office makes reference to the duty to uphold and protect the constitution and the survival of our democracy depends on upholding the constitution which it was agreed would be the foundation on which we would build our future.

As custodian of our national constitution, President Zuma has made some extraordinary public statements: *'The ANC will rule until Jesus Christ returns', 'Membership of the ANC is a ticket to heaven, those without it will land where the man with a fork is waiting'* (a reference to the devil and hell). Our constitution specifies that one of the key pillars of our democracy is that it shall be a *multiparty* democracy; citizens should be free to make political choices without the threat of hell from the custodian of our constitution.

President Zuma's statements reveal another worrying aspect of the assumptions behind the attitudes of the ANC leadership. What defines a democracy is its citizens' freedom to make choices – choices which may at some time result in a change in government through the electoral defeat of the governing party of the day. Only dictatorships coerce citizens to vote in a particular way to perpetuate their power status. The custodian of the national constitution in a democracy would be expected to encourage high quality voter education to enable citizens to make informed choices. The failure of our president to rise to this responsibility puts our democracy at risk.

Your generation has a responsibility to ensure that you become active in questioning the failure of the custodian of our constitution to uphold the key values that underpin the foundations of our democracy and you need to be robust in opposing statements that erode the values of our constitution. You also need to demand that the Independent Electoral Commission's voter education programmes go beyond the mechanics of how to vote and focus on voting as a citizen's right and responsibility that needs to be protected from coercion. We need to direct attention to the more substantive issue of the fundamental right and duty of citizens to make informed choices about who governs and how to hold those elected to government at all levels accountable for performance on election promises.

There is a subtext in post-apartheid party politics that underpins the above issues and warrants being challenged by citizens, and that is the view that the ANC as a liberation movement was solely responsible for the freedom we enjoy today and thus deserves electoral support. This view is open to challenge. Some ANC leaders go as far as telling voters that not voting for the ANC will put South Africa's democracy at risk and allow white apartheid supporters to regain power. Such views are misleading and dangerous and loom even larger in a society that has failed to provide education and training to a significant majority of its population. Uneducated people who are not easily able to analyse the political messages they receive are susceptible to accepting non-evidence based political policy approaches that may make them even more vulnerable to poverty and marginalisation. Many are dependent on social welfare and are easily misled into believing that 'delivery of services' is a favour that only party loyalists are entitled to. These are unethical and immoral views and approaches that undermine national public trust and the building of stable social relationships. Unfortunately the governing party leadership has not come forward to contradict those promoting such views.

The failure to make the transition from liberation movement to political party in a constitutional democracy is a global phenomenon. The ANC needs only to acknowledge that it has fallen into the trap of pursuing the same failed pathway that has created such devastation in post-colonial Africa because acknowledgement is an essential first step to enable us to learn from our mistakes and to forge a new pathway.

In the next chapter we will focus on an aspect of failure to govern that needs to be dealt with on its own, given the urgency of attending to it before we are plunged into crisis.

CHAPTER 5

FAILURE TO TRANSFORM THE SOCIO-ECONOMIC LANDSCAPE

The failure to transform socio-economic relations inherited from the apartheid state has made freedom an empty dream for the majority of South Africans who remain at the bottom of the socio-economic ladder. This emptiness is sadly captured by a young black man calling in on the After Eight Debate on SA FM that focused on the ANCYL leader Julius Malema's disciplinary case on 30 August 2011: 'It is good that Julius is rich, rich people do not listen to poor people like us who have nothing. They will listen to him because he is rich.' The same sentiment was expressed by the thousands of young men and women who came from many of South Africa's provinces to support Julius Malema at the ANC disciplinary hearing at Luthuli

House in Johannesburg. These young people were prepared to expose themselves to battles with the police on the streets of Johannesburg and their voices, normally unheard, were made louder by the mayhem they unleashed on police and journalists in the streets.

The Mandela and Mbeki presidencies focused on stabilising the macro-economic base of the post-apartheid economy following conventional wisdom of the 1990s informed by economists associated with what became known as the Washington Consensus. The concept and name of the Washington Consensus was first presented in 1989 by John Williamson, an economist from the Institute for International Economics, an international economic think tank based in Washington DC.[50] Williamson used the term to summarise commonly shared themes in policy advice by Washington-based institutions at the time – especially the International Monetary Fund, World Bank, and US Treasury Department – which were believed to be necessary for Latin America's recovery from the economic and financial crises of the 1980s.

The Consensus as originally stated by Williamson included ten broad sets of relatively specific policy recommendations:

1. Fiscal policy discipline, with avoidance of large fiscal deficits relative to GDP
2. Redirection of public spending from subsidies ('especially indiscriminate subsidies') towards broad-based provision of key pro-growth, pro-poor services like primary education, primary health care and infrastructure investment
3. Tax reform, broadening the tax base and adopting moderate marginal tax rates
4. Interest rates that are market determined and positive (but moderate) in real terms

5. Competitive exchange rates
6. Trade liberalisation: liberalisation of imports, with particular emphasis on elimination of quantitative restrictions (licensing, etc); any trade protection to be provided by low and relatively uniform tariffs
7. Liberalisation of inward foreign direct investment
8. Privatisation of state enterprises
9. Deregulation: abolition of regulations that impede market entry or restrict competition, except for those justified on safety, environmental and consumer protection grounds, and prudent oversight of financial institutions
10. Legal security for property rights

One cannot disagree with some of the fundamental principles of ensuring a stable macro-economic framework and fiscal discipline as essential building blocks for economic well-being. But the first question should be what kind of society would one like to establish and what kind of socio-economic relations should underpin the vision of a constitutional democracy that is united in its diversity and social justice? The failure to engage in national discussions about the nature of the socio-economic transformation we sought to establish is a major impediment to the establishment of a social justice framework as enjoined by our national constitution. The opportunity for these discussions was lost by the conscious exclusion of violations of socio-economic rights from the deliberations of the Truth and Reconciliation Commission (TRC) which focused only on gross violations of human rights. Our society remains haunted by this omission.

South Africa rightly prides itself on the success of the TRC process. But despite the heroic efforts by those citizens who contributed to the ritual forgiveness processes, the depth of resentment and mistrust in our society remains substantial. It is a deep wound that is mined skilfully by political leaders especially during election campaign periods. The fact that for strategic reasons the TRC process excluded violations of socio-economic rights left a huge burden of unresolved inequities on the backs of the poorest among us. There was no direct redress for individuals who felt wronged beyond token amounts of not more than R30 000 paid out to a fraction of those impoverished by apartheid's inequities.

The Reconstruction and Development Programme (RDP) that was to have provided housing, water and sanitation, education and health care for poor people was neither successful nor sustained long enough to adequately address the vast needs left in the wake of so many decades of neglect. The political philosophy of the government undervalued partnerships between the government, the private sector and civil society and discouraged any collaborative work that could have contributed to tackling the massive socio-economic backlog. Instead, the RDP became part and parcel of the patronage of the ruling party dished out to loyal party cadres regardless of competence or capacity to execute. We are now faced with the huge problem of growing inequality between those who do not have access to basic infrastructure and public services on one hand, and those who have made the transition into middle class status on the other.

The ANC political machinery has become adept at playing victim of apartheid and not taking responsibility for its failures. This has become the reason for failure to transform apartheid's socio-economic inequities and for the poor performance of successive post-apartheid administrations in measures to eradicate poverty. Voters who stand to gain most from successful, more efficient and effective governance are the very ones who are easily mobilised to continue to support the liberation movement-linked ANC despite its failures. The 2011 local elections showed a very ugly side of this blame game when voters were told only about the successes of the ANC and the risks that they faced if they voted for other parties not committed to the ideals of freedom.

An example of the ANC's failure to deliver on its promises is in the provision of housing, which successive ANC administrations have none the less touted as a success. However, the National Home Builders Registration Council reported in 2011 that of the just over 3 million RDP houses built, 2.6 million or 87 per cent were unsafe for those living in them. It estimated that a total of R59 billion was needed to remedy both minor and major defects in these houses. This is the cost of giving tenders to build houses for poor people to politically connected people with limited skills. It further demonstrates how corruption is a tax on poor people who have to forgo basic services and better quality accommodation because money is being diverted into the pockets of those who have captured the state for their own interests. There is no report of any of those involved in these tenders being held to account for failure to perform.

Related to the housing issue is the provision of basic services including water, electricity and sanitation. The ANC made much of the inequity of the Makhaza open toilet saga in Khayelitsha as an example of the Democratic Alliance's (DA) racist allocation of resources in Cape Town. No one can justify 51 open toilets even if one could argue about the details of the Makhaza case. The fact that Andile Lindi, a member of the ANCYL, was the consultant of Kula Development, the company responsible for executing the Cape Town project in Khayelitsha, is no excuse for the DA-governed city to allow toilets of the indigent residents to remain open until the incident was brought to light. But when the scandal of 1600 open toilets in the Rammulotsi Township in Viljoenskroon came to light just a week before the May 2011 local elections, the ANC at first denied knowing about them, then the Free State secretary general of the ANC admitted that they had become aware of them in July 2010. It will be interesting to see whether the threat of 'heads will roll' becomes a reality in a political party that has no track record of letting heads roll for poor performance in public service.

Successive post-colonial African governments have resorted to blaming others for their failure to govern. First it was the neo-colonials and Cold War contestants who were responsible for our failures by making us into clientele states. Then it was the World Bank and the International Monetary Fund with their structural adjustment programmes and the Washington Consensus that forced austerity measures on hapless economies. Now it is 'the West' with its 'regime change' agenda trying to unseat African political leaders it does not like and undermining 'African solutions for African problems'. At what stage are African governments going to accept responsibility for their performance in governance, both good and bad?

South Africa is proving incapable of escaping the trap of bad governance. It has followed the flawed model of turning the ANC as a liberation movement into a governing party without giving any attention to the fundamental change in its ethos. The dysfunctional nature of its internal governance systems is spilling over into the wider national governance domain. The Tripartite Alliance with the trade union movement COSATU on one hand, and the SACP on the other, has merely complicated the degree of dysfunctional governance systems in our democracy. COSATU and the SACP's blind support of workers' rights with no reference to their responsibility to perform has undermined any attempt to hold teachers, nurses and other public sector workers accountable for their performance in key areas of the nation's life.

It comes as no surprise that our health, education and social development sectors have been undermined by inappropriate policies, ineffective leadership and management, as well as political bargaining within the governing party's Tripartite Alliance. Successive post-apartheid presidents have failed to understand the importance of the social sectors as a foundation for developing and enhancing the human capabilities that are essential to successful democracies and economies in the twenty-first century. The view seems to be that anyone can head these sectors. Inadequate strategic leadership coupled with low political priority attached to their outcomes and the enormous legacy issues embedded within these sectors have rendered them the weakest ministries since 1994.

Transforming apartheid's socio-economic legacy would be a massive task in anyone's estimation. Reconstructing and developing a new social framework and human settlement pattern is a gigantic challenge which has been underestimated by the successive post-apartheid administrations and unfortunately 70 to 80 per cent of the population bears the brunt of the underperformance of the social sectors, leading to growing inequality in our society and the persistence of apartheid's geography.

Let us look at the state of our public health system which was crippled by the deployment of non-health sector trained personnel in management positions under the presidency of Thabo Mbeki. The breakdown in management under Members of the Executive Committee (MECs) and superintendents of hospitals who had no understanding of how the health system works left a trail of disasters which resulted in the unnecessary deaths of vulnerable people. It is mind boggling that a teacher with no training or experience in the health sector was made Head of the Department of Health in one of the poorest provinces – but that is the reality that poor people have to contend with in 2012 post-apartheid South Africa.

In the second half of 2011, the Development Bank of Southern Africa published the report of a study commissioned by the Minister of Health, Dr Aaron Motsoaledi. This study found that major health facilities, including tertiary hospitals, were headed by CEOs who had no experience of health systems. Many had qualifications in health administration which are largely theoretical courses that do not adequately prepare their holders for the logistical and technical challenges of running a modern health facility. Some CEOs were nurses who had a limited understanding of the complex scientific requirements of tertiary health care systems.[51] The result of these misguided appointments has been a decline in the quality of public health services with devastating consequences for poor people.

Other reasons for our dysfunctional public sector are the number of vacancies and the misalignment between those deployed to positions and their capacities to execute the assigned responsibilities. The widespread nature of the problem is illustrated in reports from the Auditor-General:[52]

- All national departments had an average vacancy rate of 18 per cent with the highest being 46 per cent in the Department of Water Affairs. Approximately 19 per cent of the positions for senior managers and highly skilled staff were vacant.

Conversations with My Sons and Daughters

- Furthermore, the Auditor General reported that 11 departments were not complying with acceptable time frames and only 5 of those had reported (as they are required to do) on the reasons for their non-compliance.
- At times officials were requested to act in more senior positions than those for which they were qualified, but not for periods exceeding 12 months, yet instances were found where officials were receiving acting allowances beyond the 12-month cut-off point. It was pointed out that 'prolonged acting periods can be an indication of ineffective processes to appoint or recruit suitable permanent staff'.
- The selection processes for personnel have specific procedures for verifying criminal and financial/asset records, citizenship, financial status, qualifications and previous employment, but the report found evidence that they were not being followed at all in some departments (eg Defence, The Presidency and Public Works) while the processes were incomplete in other departments (eg Water Affairs, Home Affairs, Health, Human Settlements).

The skills and competency discrepancies in our public sector become worse as one gets closer to the citizen. At the national level, the departments closest to people, especially vulnerable poor people, such as Education, Health, Social Development and Correctional Services, are often run by poorly equipped people at the operational levels. Provincial and local authority structures are frequently found to have inadequate governance processes in place resulting in ineffectual performance that robs the majority of South Africans of their basic needs entitlements. Poor people are thus trapped in poverty due to an ineffectual and unaccountable government.

The disparity between the ideals spelt out in our national constitution, which was negotiated under the watchful eye of Nelson Mandela, and our present reality is growing, attesting further to the failure of the ANC to make the transition from liberation movement to political party in a democratic system where there is open competition for power. Competition for the spoils of freedom is becoming more intense within the ANC as increasing numbers of struggle comrades feel that they have lost out. Access to power, the tried and tested way to prosperity, is hotly contested. The overall effects of the non-performance of the governing party is becoming obvious to all and is beginning to evoke desperation and rebellion among poor communities who have none the less undeniably been the pillars of the ANC's electoral majorities. Sustainability of the hegemony of the ANC may become an issue in years to come as internal and external pressures mount.

The SAIRR Fast Facts reports that in October 2010, in his medium-term budget review, the Minister of Finance, Pravin Gordhan, said that government agencies were investigating fraudulent tenders valued at R25 billion. The Special Investigating Unit (SIU) estimates that 20 to 25 per cent of state procurement expenditure, amounting to roughly R30 billion, is lost to overpayment or theft every year.

Fraud and corruption seem particularly rife in the government's low-cost housing initiative, where contracts worth R2 billion are being probed. More than 1 540 cases of fraud involving some R850 million in social grants in KwaZulu-Natal alone were reported to the police in an 18-month period. Some ministers have abused public revenues to fund lavish lifestyles. For instance, Sicelo Shiceka, Minister of Traditional Affairs and Co-operative Governance, spent more than R335 000 on a visit to Switzerland to see a girlfriend in prison while claiming to be on official 'World Cup duties'. He was dismissed in October 2011 after the Public Protector found him guilty of dishonesty and the abuse of public resources.

Corruption is also evident in the irregular leasing of office premises for government departments, often at inflated rentals and without proper tender procedures. This issue came sharply into focus in August 2010, when the *Sunday Times* reported that the National Commissioner of Police, General Bheki Cele, had breached tender rules in approving a R500 million lease for new office accommodation for the police in Pretoria. The Public Protector, Ms Thuli Madonsela, confirmed that General Cele's conduct was unlawful, but it took more than two months after she handed over her full report to President Zuma for action to be taken against Cele and Gwen Nkabinde-Mahlangu. Both were found to have acted unlawfully in allocating a tender to lease two premises, one in Pretoria and the other in Durban, to politically connected businessman Roux Shabangu at inflated rates. Nkabinde-Mahlangu, then Minister of Public Works, was dismissed in October 2011. Bheki Cele was suspended that same month and was finally axed by President Zuma in June 2012. The culture of impunity that seemed to have underpinned these two leases and the complete disregard of cost to the taxpayer exemplify the extent to which public officials feel entitled to do as they please.

The governing party's tolerance of corrupt behaviour violates all rules for the accountability of public servants. An increasing number of public servants, who have been accused and in many cases been found guilty of wrong-doing for their disregard of proper public conduct and accountability, are being rewarded with senior posts, which seems to convey the message that as long as the governing party accepts you as a worthy and loyal member, wrong-doing is of no consequence. The issue of entitlement that seems to be at the heart of the brazen widespread corruption within our public service is a cause for concern, as the ANC seems to regard the state as a source of patronage for its members, regardless of the impact on socio-economic outcomes for poor people. Such practices give credence to Moeletsi Mbeki's charge that African leaders are 'architects of poverty' – a logical outcome of the unaccountable politics that results from disengaged citizens.

The question that demands an answer is why the electorate continues to tolerate this level of impunity by the ruling party. Why are South African citizens so married to a party that has shown scant respect for them as the sovereigns of a constitutional democracy? Why do poor people vote in the same public representatives who ignore them after elections? More specifically, why do you, as young well-informed citizens, not raise your voices and use the power of your vote to effect change in the accountability systems of our country?

———————

Let us consider now the missed opportunities of regional economic integration in Africa. Regional integration is a key feature for a successful African Renaissance that would see Africa leveraging its youthful population, its vast land mass and its unmatched mineral resources to trade and grow itself into a serious global economic power. To this end, South Africa played a seminal role in developing and promoting the New Partnership for Africa's Development (NEPAD) under President Thabo Mbeki. There has, however, been little progress made in achieving such integration in Africa during the last decade and intra-Africa trade remains insignificant at around 10 per cent compared to 60 per cent, 40 per cent and 30 per cent intra-regional trade that have been achieved by Europe, North America and ASEAN respectively.[53]

Post-colonial Africa's failure to collaborate as a region in an increasingly competitive global economy is sadly reflected by the failure of SADC as the most powerful sub-region to set the tone and lead by example. South African leaders over the last eighteen years have failed to enable a capable SADC sub-regional economic machinery and have played along with the age-old practice of appointing a secretariat that is drawn from member government non-meritocratic bureaucracies. The result has been paralysis, inefficiency and disappointment. There is also the matter of overlapping membership of sub-regional bodies with some countries being members of both SADC and the Common Market of Southern Africa (COMESA).

While it has often been suggested that these two organisations would be better off if they were to merge, the matter has proved to be very politically sensitive. Efforts have been made to coordinate the work of the two organisations in order to prevent duplication and conflict of their programmes, projects and activities and since 2001 they have been cooperating in a number of areas such as trade analytical work, capacity building and negotiations, transport issues and international relations such as preparations for and negotiations with the European Union and the World Trade Organisation.[54]

African countries have struggled to develop credible migration policies to reassure their citizens that border security imperatives are balanced with the need for Africa to attract and retain its talent pool within the continent in order to drive its economic and social development. The Economic Commission for Africa (ECA) estimates that between 1960 and 1989, some 127 000 highly qualified African professionals left the continent. According to the International Organisation for Migration (IOM), Africa has been losing 20 000 professionals each year since 1990. This trend has sparked claims that the continent is dying a slow death from brain drain, and belated recognition by the United Nations that the 'emigration of African professionals to the West is one of the greatest obstacles to Africa's development'.

Brain drain in Africa has financial, institutional, and societal costs. African countries get little return from their investment in higher education, since too many graduates leave or fail to return home at the end of their studies. In light of a dwindling professional sector, African institutions are increasingly dependent on foreign expertise. To fill the human resource gap created by brain drain, Africa employs up to 150 000 expatriate professionals at a cost of US$4 billion a year.[55]

South Africa has failed to leverage its position as the strongest African economy and be the welcoming destination for those who are pushed into leaving their countries by adverse political and economic circumstances. We could learn from countries such as the USA, Canada and Australia about how to turn immigrants into a powerful tool to win the talent war for skills and innovators. These countries have immigration regimes that are geared to serving the interests of their economies and higher education institutions. The immigration ministries are an essential part of the economic and trade strategic clusters to ensure the supply of adequate skills. Skilled people are the sustaining job creators in any economy, yet South Africa makes their immigration harder than any other middle income country. How do we expect to fill the 800 000 skilled job vacancies that are slowing down our ability to grow and create jobs? You, as young professionals, need to challenge your government to stop sabotaging our economic prosperity.

Our inability to run a proper refugee programme that would enable skilled refugees to be placed in areas of critical skills shortages has created a lose-lose scenario. South Africa is host to millions of refugees who are prevented from being value-adders and instead have to eke out an existence in ways that often put a strain on our public services and create conflict with the poorest citizens who become resentful of foreigners. South Africa is a magnet for desperate Africans fleeing poverty and despotic governments. We have to accept this and turn it into an opportunity to source valuable skills and to establish links with those who might later return to their countries and promote trade with us.

South Africa is in denial about the horrific attacks on foreign nationals of African descent in recent times. These attacks are the result of the government's failure to articulate a clear migration policy, to fulfil its primary role of securing our borders and to take corrective action in the light of weaknesses in both policy making and implementation. Some South Africans believe that foreigners are usurping the opportunities and services meant for them. In addition, public service delivery failures by government which have led to protests by affected citizens often result in the targeting of foreign nationals in their neighbourhoods and the destruction and looting of foreign-owned businesses.[56] Failure of leadership has led to poor people taking the law into their own hands and settling scores they feel the government is failing to address. Our reputation as a country with a human rights based national constitution has been severely dented by government failures in this regard.

Urgent action is needed to address the reality of South Africa's being a magnet for both political and economic refugees. Asylum seekers cannot just be left to fend for themselves in competition with citizens at the bottom of the socio-economic pyramid of our unequal society. Competition for scarce resources as well as envy directed at more resourceful and successful migrants is inevitable in such an environment.

You, as future leaders, need to assume your responsibilities to understand these interconnected challenges and become advocates of change towards a more realistic, human rights based and ultimately creative way of repositioning South Africa as the sought after destination for talented young Africans. Your generation stands to gain from being more connected with your own continent which is amongst the fastest growing regions in the world with a huge mineral, natural and human resource base that is the envy of the rest of the world.

CHAPTER 6

BETRAYAL OF FUTURE GENERATIONS

The monumental failure to successfully transform our education system undermines any effort to promote a more equitable society. President John F Kennedy of the USA once said: 'Our progress as a nation can be no swifter than our progress in education. The human mind is our fundamental resource.'[57] Our failure is a betrayal of the generation of young people who on 16 June 1976 stood up to a brutal apartheid regime and refused to continue to be subjected to 'gutter education'. Theirs was a revolt against inferior education as a pillar of divisive social engineering focused on ensuring that black people would not become a competitive threat to white dominance. The apartheid government feared that should black people have access to equal education, they might outperform white people in the professional, technical and other areas where job reservation protected them from competition.

One cannot but agree with the statement in the National Planning Commission (NPC) Diagnostic Review published in mid-2011 that: 'One of apartheid's greatest crimes was the provision of substandard education to black people.' The NPC goes on to admit that: 'Efforts (by post-apartheid governments) to raise the quality of education for poor children have largely failed.' The critical question is what is the cause of this failure? Should we not be asking ourselves as citizens of a democratic South Africa why successive post-apartheid governments are continuing to commit the same crime against the majority of children today? Why are we so tolerant of the fact that 80 per cent of schools serving largely black children are dysfunctional? Why are we passive witnesses of the destruction of opportunities of successive generations of children by an education and training system based on low expectations of what our children can achieve?

The NPC states the obvious: school performance is crucially linked to the role of teachers, principals and parents. Studies from other countries suggest that teacher performance and the quality of school leadership are the key variables to success in improving quality of schooling. In our situation the performance of teachers is hampered by many factors, not least of which are absenteeism and poor content knowledge of the subjects they are teaching. According to the Southern and East African Consortium of Monitoring Educational Quality (SACMEQIII), teachers struggle with such basic issues as calculating percentages. For example, more than half the teachers tested thought that if the height of a fence is raised from 60 centimetres to 75 centimetres, that represented a 15 per cent increase. 'It also shows that teachers have problems with relatively simple maths problems,' says Servaas van den Berg.[58]

A 2010 study comparing the performance of South African primary schools in the North West Province with that of our neighbour, Botswana, provides further evidence of the gap between South African children's schooling experience and that of their peers in the region. Botswana's 13 000 primary school teachers for 330 000 pupils are trained for three years at government teacher training colleges, whereas South Africa's 27 226 teachers for about 13 million[59] pupils are trained at Schools of Education within universities or universities of technology. There is not much significant difference between the two countries in the length of training and qualifications.

Nine thousand Grade 6 learners on either side of the border were tested twice: at the beginning of the academic year and at the end of it. It was found that learners in Botswana scored significantly higher on the initial test and made significant gains over the academic year. Both teachers and pupils in South Africa showed a lack of content knowledge of basic mathematics and statistics. Batswana teachers taught a minimum of 60 per cent of the mathematics curriculum compared to South African teachers who covered only 40 per cent of the curriculum. South African teachers said: 'We bunk classes because we don't like teaching, and we don't like it because we are not confident, and we are not confident because we are not trained in the subject.'[60] Why are you part of the conspiracy of silence in the face of betrayal of generations of children entrusted to these teachers?

A Human Sciences Research Council (HSRC) study quoted by the NPC Diagnostic Report found that 20 per cent of teachers are absent on Mondays and Fridays and absentee rates increase to a third at month-end. Teachers in schools serving poor African pupils teach an average of 3.5 hours per day compared to 6.5 hours in former white schools, which now serve largely middle and upper-class pupils. Time lost by poor black pupils over the 12-year period of schooling amounts to three years. Three years of lost time on the task for learning is a major contributor to lower quality outcomes for black school leavers for it is difficult to imagine how they could make up for it. It explains why they underperform compared with their peers at former white schools, known as Model C schools.[61] This underperformance lies at the heart of the growing gap between poor black pupils and their middle and upper-class counterparts – both black and white – in terms of access to higher education and training as well as job opportunities. This is yet another example of our silent complicity to the irresponsibility of teachers who are paid for doing nothing and in the process are extinguishing the dreams of so many young people.

Instead of tackling this chronic underperformance in the majority of our schools, our education officials opted for lower standards of performance. The bar between success and failure is set so low that young people do not have to exert themselves to succeed. How else can one explain setting 30 per cent in three subjects and 40 per cent in another three as the qualification for a high school diploma? This standard condones failure to demonstrate mastery over fully 70 per cent and 60 per cent of the knowledge base of the chosen high school subjects as acceptable. We are destroying the seeds of the future of our country by making underperformance part of the institutional culture of our education system.

These low standards become even more alarming when looked at in combination with low curriculum demands. For example, we seem to have made the assumption that schoolchildren should not be stretched to learn to understand the language of mathematics and science. We assume that these subjects are too difficult for them. What is the basis of this assumption? We also see nothing wrong in letting children go through school without learning about the history of their own country, let alone that of Africa and the wider world. How are these children to understand why things are what they are and how are they to learn about what changes have brought us to where we are and what lessons we can learn from that history? The failure to inculcate the love of reading and writing as well as appreciation of literature in both mother tongue and second languages has led to millions of young people being underprepared for the world of the twenty-first century. It is tragic that South Africa has failed to take advantage of its sophisticated infrastructure to use information technology to accelerate teaching and learning. Poorer countries such as Rwanda are far ahead of us in using ICT in both education and in conducting the business of government.

Experience worldwide points to the capacity of children to rise to the expectations set for them in an environment that encourages and rewards effort and innovation. Even in our own country, 600 of the total of more than 26 000 public schools consistently outperform their peers to produce close to 100 per cent pass rates and higher maths and science outcomes. The key difference between these 600 high-performing schools and the rest is in the quality of leadership and teaching, with leadership ensuring discipline in the classroom and in the conduct of both teachers and learners.

So why is it difficult for the government to make sure that teachers are in class on time and using appropriate teaching aids, despite President Zuma's promises to ensure this? Unionisation of more than 80 per cent of teachers over the last three decades is a major factor in the underperformance of the school system. The South African Democratic Teachers Union (SADTU) is the largest union with over 240 000 of the total of close to 400 000 teachers in the country. It is a COSATU affiliate and thus part of the Tripartite Alliance that is governing the country together with the ANC and the SACP. Their attitude to absenteeism is in radical contrast to that of the second largest teacher union, the National Professional Teachers Organisation of South Africa (NAPTOSA). SADTU's view is 'We encourage our members to be at school on time but there is time given out (by schools) for us for union work. We do advise them (teachers) to remain on board.' NAPTOSA, on the other hand is quite clear: 'Members engaging in union work during school teaching hours is behaviour we totally discourage. The time when the teacher is in front of the class is sacred.'

The conclusion is inescapable that unionism is the major focus for SADTU, regardless of what impact it might have on learning and teaching. As one of its leaders said: 'The day our militancy stops so will our existence.' NAPTOSA's focus is on professionalism and the sacred duty of teaching. Teachers in South Africa are amongst the highest paid in the world, yet gross underperformance that undermines our ability to develop high levels of skills and human capability is tolerated by our government. It can only be inferred that the block vote that SADTU represents is the impediment to the ANC government's exercising its role of holding these public servants accountable. The losers are the 13 million children who leave the school system every twelve-year school cycle without the requisite preparation for life in the twenty-first century.

To add insult to injury, Umalusi, the National Examination Standard Moderator, decided to adjust the final marks of the 2010 matriculation results upwards despite teaching time (more than three weeks) being lost to the World Soccer Cup and the teachers' strike that followed. It came as a surprise to many analysts that with so much time lost to the teaching and learning process, the matriculation pass rate actually increased from 61 per cent in 2009 to 67 per cent in 2010. Either time on the task does not matter in terms of education outcomes, or something else is at play here. Umalusi, under pressure from education experts and analysts released the details of the adjustments in late February 2011.[62]

	2010	2009	2008
Mathematics	38%	27.3%	28.26%
Life Sciences	38%	34.84%	35.1%
Geography	34.80%	35.07%	35.80%
Accounting	33%	32%	33%
Physical Science	30.26%	25.17%	30.33%

We should be more outraged by the national average marks attained by successive cohorts of high school graduates in key subjects rather than by the quantum of adjustments, disturbing as these are. How in the world are we going to function as a society with the overwhelming majority of our children performing at this appalling level in those subjects most essential to modern socio-economic competence? To add to the crisis, performance in the languages was not much better either. Our children are being denied the opportunities to develop into well-rounded, literate, numerate and critical thinking citizens. Why are we as South African citizens allowing this to continue on our watch?

The inescapable conclusion is that those in government and the agencies involved in setting curricula and standards and norms of performance are driven by the fear of failure. What this says is that we have little confidence in our children's capacities to perform at the level required by the demanding knowledge-driven global community of which we are a part. The low expectations we have of our children is a consequence of our own lack of self-confidence which we are perpetuating in future generations. This intergenerational lack of confidence generates a vicious cycle that condemns the majority of our society to mediocrity with devastating repercussions for the country's capacity to compete with its peers in the global economy.

The most fundamental measure of a decent society is reflected in the quality of life of its children. The commitment to make sure that children have better opportunities than previous generations to develop their capabilities and performance as human beings is also a key indicator of the values of a successful society. Every indicator in our society points to a regression in the quality of life of our children, especially for those at the bottom of the socio-economic ladder.

For example, infant and child mortality rates are rising, with UNICEF estimating that in 2010 there were 58 000 deaths of children under the age of five years in South Africa.[63] Research[64] has shown that thousands of deaths of mothers and babies can be prevented at district hospital level, where little has changed since an audit of 34 such facilities five years ago. South Africa would be able to get back on track if it boosted a few carefully selected high-impact interventions upon which a new government plan was based. These included increasing the effective implementation of basic neonatal care and boosting dual therapy prevention of mother-to-child HIV transmission programmes (with appropriate feeding choices) to 95 per cent coverage. The interventions would also avert many maternal deaths and stillbirths at a cost of 24 per cent of the public sector health expenditure with an incremental cost of R1.6 billion per year. Such progress would put South Africa 'squarely on track' to meet Millennium Development Goal (MDG) 4 (reducing by two-thirds the mortality rate among children under five), and possibly MDG 5 (reducing by three-quarters the maternal mortality rate). 'The costs are affordable and the key gap is leadership and effective implementation at every level of the health system, including national and local accountability for service provision.'

The delay in the government response to HIV/AIDS has created a major strain on our society and its fabric. Children growing up without the benefit of parental love and guidance are at huge risk of falling prey to social ills. The number of double orphans is increasing and in 2010 was estimated as more than 10 million in sub-Saharan Africa. An interesting UNICEF study found that just under 60 per cent of double orphans lost both their parents between the ages of five and nine.[65]

Teenage pregnancy is on the rise and child abuse and forced under-age marriages are increasing, especially in rural areas. The composite estimates for the period indicate that there was a decline in teenage fertility throughout the 1980s, followed by a spike in the early 1990s which coincided with the political transition taking place in the country at the time, followed by a sustained decline in teenage fertility until 2005. These trends were verified by a demographic surveillance site – Africa Centre for Health and Population Studies in rural KwaZulu-Natal.[66]

UNICEF 2010 data estimates that 4 per cent of female adolescents aged between 15 and 19 years are currently married/in union.[67]

This regression is all the more worrying because our government not only committed itself to promote the rights of the child as enshrined in our national constitution, but also continues to commit fiscal resources to advance the progressive realisation of socio-economic rights. The gap between commitment and performance reflects a deep-seated crisis of execution by our government in areas critical for the development of human capability and capacity to live in the twenty-first century.

We are failing to live up to our national system of values at all levels of children's developmental path – the home, community, school and wider society – and this has become a vicious cycle that is undermining our future as a society. Children who are not nurtured and socialised into believing that they are valued, loved and respected often fail to grow up into young people with the capabilities and capacities to fulfil the roles of citizenship and responsible adulthood.

Our government recognises that education is the sure and tested way out of poverty and this is reflected in education being the recipient of the largest slice of the government budget – 21 per cent of the R979 billion 2011/12 budget. The key to the underperformance of our education system is the quality and motivation of our teachers for no system of education can function well with largely underqualified, demoralised and ill-disciplined teachers. Our education system is deteriorating despite the commitments of the ANC 10 Point Plan[68] for improving the performance of education, the first of which calls on 'Teachers to be in Class, on Time and Teaching Using Textbooks'! One might well ask what else teachers are supposed to do? Why would this injunction be necessary in any system of education worth its salt?

The continuing underperformance of our education system has a disproportionate effect on poor people. The majority of the 40 per cent of young people between the ages of 18 and 35 years who are unskilled and unemployed are black and poor. They are the drop-outs from our wasteful school system which has shed almost two-thirds of each age cohort of close to 1.5 million who start Grade 1 each year for much of the last decade or so. By the time the final matriculation examinations are written, only just more than half a million present themselves. Successful candidates have consistently been under 70 per cent of the total who sit for the examinations, despite the lowering of standards for success to a 30 per cent pass in three subjects and a 40 per cent pass in three others. Our education system is probably the most wasteful in the world. Why are we so tolerant of this waste?

There is a direct correlation between the performance of our education and training systems and the level of skills shortages and unemployment amongst the youth. We should heed Malcolm Gladwell's advice borrowing an Asian proverb that: 'No one who can rise before dawn three hundred sixty days a year fails to make his family rich'.[69] Gladwell goes on to demonstrate that the so-called Asian aptitude for mathematics is a product of a culture of effort facilitated by the structure of Asian languages. Asian schools are at work for more days in the year than many other countries, including the USA; the school year in South Korea is 220 days, in Japan it is 243 days, while in the USA it is only 180 days. In addition, Asian languages use easier configurations to compute numbers in a more logical fashion than English and other western language derivatives. Gladwell writes that

> If you speak English, you have about a 50 per cent chance of remembering that sequence perfectly. If you're Chinese, though, you're almost certain to get it right every time. Why is that? Because as human beings we store digits in a memory loop that runs for about

two seconds. We most easily memorise whatever we can say or read within that two second span. And Chinese speakers get that list of numbers – 4,8,5,3,9,7,6 – right every time because – unlike English speakers – their language allows them to fit all those seven numbers into two seconds.[70]

Time on task rather than three months of summer holidays, as is the case in the USA, makes a huge difference to the performance of schoolchildren. Schools in the USA inner cities that adopt a routine of more time on the task of learning from 7.25am until 7pm every school day have shown much improvement over the years. Can you imagine our unionised teachers applying themselves in this way? No. But teachers at the 600 public schools in poor areas of South Africa, including Mbili School in Limpopo Province, are doing just this in addition to offering Saturday school for those needing to catch up on areas of challenge in the curriculum.

The conclusion is inevitable that, contrary to the apartheid government's fear of the capacity of black people to compete successfully with white people, the post-apartheid government has demonstrated its lack of confidence in black people's ability to rise to the intellectual challenge posed by high educational standards. This lack of confidence extends to low expectations of our teachers' abilities to perform to the highest professional standards. The culture of low expectation breeds low performance. It is a cruel irony that after being treated as inferior by white people, our government seems to have bought into the lie that black people cannot attain the high standards one expects of any professional. Black people, especially poor ones, are being treated as intellectually inferior to others sectors of society. People treated as inferior tend to lose respect for themselves and those close to them, initiating a cycle of humiliation, passive aggression and abusive relationships. The lack of professional conduct of teachers in poor performing schools is a reflection of this cycle.

A second conclusion one can draw is that the ANC's focus on retaining power rather than delivering on the promises of freedom has undermined the values so dear to our society. A major problem stems from not following the injunctions of our national constitution that the public service should be professional and execute its responsibilities without fear or favour. Importantly, Chapter 10 197 (3) states that 'no employee of the Public Service may be favoured or prejudiced only because that person supports a particular political party'. The reality of the everyday experience of citizens is that loyalty to the party rather than competence and ethical behaviour in line with the national constitution is the most important consideration in accessing and retaining jobs in our public service. Defiance of the basic pillars of our democracy has become part of the evolving political culture over the last decade or so.

It is understandable that any political party in power anywhere in the world would want to have loyal and trusted people to execute its policy objectives. In our situation, the ANC as the governing party has to deal with the complexities imposed by the legacy which denied the majority population access to education, training and opportunities to gain the experience needed for these tasks. How could the ANC be seen to be employing a majority of white people in the public service who would most likely qualify for positions because they have the advantage of history on their side? But the dilemma of the legacy of deliberately disadvantaging the majority population is no excuse for appointing incompetent people to critical areas in government, including all levels of the Department of Education. There are people within the ANC who are overlooked in favour of those who are less competent but are regarded as more loyal to those in power. In addition, there are qualified black people who are not aligned to any political party who are not necessarily treated with fairness in competing for jobs within the public service.

The conclusion is inescapable that being a member of the ANC is a necessary although not necessarily a sufficient condition for access to opportunities in the public service. It is proximity to power that is the essential element to success in securing such employment. It is not just who you know within the party; it is whether those you know are close enough to the right people in the right faction within the ANC. This approach to public service appointments and promotions has introduced instability and insecurity which inevitably undermine the performance of the government. The greater the competition for power within the ANC, the more one can expect instability and insecurity to increase, with tragic consequences for our society.

The dominance of personalised power within our governance system has undermined institution building at most levels of government. Institution building and enhancement are essential for good governance, transparency and accountability and require a focus on the vision we have as a society and the national goals we set for ourselves as a people. Our vision to be an egalitarian constitutional democracy in which all citizens will exercise their rights and rise to their responsibilities can only become a reality if our institutions support and promote the journey towards that future. Our system of education is failing to meet its obligations to that vision. This is a betrayal of current and future generations of children which means only one thing: ultimately it is our future that is being betrayed.

CHAPTER 7

ARE WE SUBJECTS OR CITIZENS?

No democracy can thrive without the active participation of its citizens, but the last eighteen years of post-apartheid governance have been characterised by a disengaged citizenry. There can be no other explanation for a governing party that has by its own admission failed to perform in fundamental and critical areas – such as education – to have been repeatedly returned to power with such large majorities, all above 60 per cent. Few, if any, governing parties in multiparty democracies would have survived beyond the first or at best the second election. Yet the ANC has survived three national elections despite its underperformance. How is this possible?

The simplest reason may be that the majority of South Africans lack experience of what democratic governance should be. Our experience prior to 1994 was being ruled as subjects rather than participating in governance as citizens. We have yet to shed the identity of being subjects under indigenous traditional African governance, colonial governance and apartheid governance. Our identity as citizens has yet to manifest in our attitudes to the rights and responsibilities we assumed on the dawn of our democracy and our inability to hold successive administrations accountable is an indicator of how far we still are from being engaged citizens.

The reality of governing a sophisticated constitutional democracy requires much more attention to the relationship between state and citizen than has been shown during the last eighteen years. The practice of democracy was new to all South Africans in 1994, yet to date little consideration has been given to educating for democracy. The complementary roles of citizens, the governing party, the president, the government and the state are not understood by the majority, especially those who lack education or have not been exposed to models of democracy elsewhere.

Conversations about the importance of engaged citizenry were strengthened in 2009 by the release of the report of the Dinokeng Scenarios[71] on our country's possible future. The process was sponsored by Old Mutual and Nedbank out of concern that the glow of the political settlement of 1994 was fading. The Scenario Team was drawn from political party circles, from independent citizens with no party affiliations, from the private and public sectors as well as from civil society organisations. Despite the diversity of their backgrounds, the Team soon found themselves developing consensus about the nature of the challenges facing our society as well as their root causes. The challenges were summarised as:

- poor educational and training outcomes;
- high levels of unemployment, especially amongst the youth;
- a poorly functioning health system and high levels of HIV/AIDS;
- high levels of crime and insecurity.

The process of the meeting of minds, encouraged by the symbolism of the confluence of rivers – *Dinokeng* – was ably facilitated by Adam Kahane supported by Ishmael Mkhabela.[72] It was not an easy process nor was the venue in a tent city a comfortable one. The landscape off the infamous Moloto Road is rugged bushveld with some lovely hills inhabited by a small population of wildlife: giraffes, springboks, and other grazers. For those afraid of creepy crawlies there was no place to hide and we were repeatedly warned about the presence of snakes. Walking to and from our tents required an escort by security personnel with torches to illuminate the footpaths.

But the most challenging aspect of the process was building trust within the Team across the barriers of party politics and ideologies. At the first workshop in August 2007 the tensions that pervaded the conversations and the body language of the participants could be cut with a knife. The pre-Polokwane blues created tensions between ANC members participating in the workshop – the lines were drawn between those for and those against the nomination of Jacob Zuma as president of the ANC. But even among those who shared views about whether or not President Thabo Mbeki was to be succeeded by Jacob Zuma, mistrust was palpable and visible. Someone captured the emerging culture within the governing party as 'no different from that of hyena pups who kill their siblings to secure themselves a larger share of the diminishing flow of their mother's milk'.

Ideological divisions were most stark between the Afriforum members and those of liberation movement origins, reaching a point where one participant said that convergence was impossible because at the end of the day the conflict was about competition for scarce resources. The zero sum notion of power was clearly the operating principle here. The idea that power can be shared as a public good is not a commonly held view, for the more one does so by enabling others to become active agents of their own development, the more one contributes to enlarging the resource base. The zero-sum notion of power blinds its adherents to this enriching possibility. Not even the ice-breaking circle in which we introduced ourselves and brought a symbol of what matters to each of us, could reduce the level of mistrust and tension.

In a stroke of brilliance, the facilitators broke the tension by sending us in smaller groups to visit various places: orphanages, a local prison, a woman community innovator named Mmatshepo, a meeting of a proposed Big Five project in the area, Cullinan – a former De Beers mining operation famous for the discovery of one of the world's largest diamonds, the Cullinan Diamond. Each of these places forced us to reflect on the reality of life in our beloved country. For example, we witnessed a successful prison management programme focused on correctional support rather than punishment of inmates. The transformative leadership of Mmatshepo ('mother of hope'), a former nurse who pioneered healing through eco-agriculture among mentally ill patients to whom she used to dispense drugs, was another wake-up call for our Team. Mmatshepo decided decades ago to stop dispensing pills; instead she encouraged her patients to plant the seeds she distributed by working with them directly.

She has evolved into a resource which helps local farmers to rethink sustainable agriculture by embracing eco/organic methodologies.

Another project visited by participants showcased the generosity of a retired couple who provide a loving transitional home for abandoned children on their smallholding based on their trust that they were doing God's work and He would therefore provide for the needs of the home. We also witnessed how racism remains a trap among the white farming community that was meeting to plan for a Big Five wildlife project where they would pool their farms with the Gauteng provincial government. When asked what the role of the local community would be in this project they found it difficult to conceive of a partnership with the local black people, other than as 'hewers of wood'.

Sharing these stories as a Team enabled us to move beyond our own rigid views about social relationships shaped by notions of race, class and gender. We were forced to confront the complexities of our realities that defined our stereotypical views and were in a sense reintroduced to our country's realities. It took many more weekends (four in all), role plays, games, conversations and more conversations for the Team to come to a consensus. The Dinokeng Scenario Team painted the possible future of our country in the following diagram:

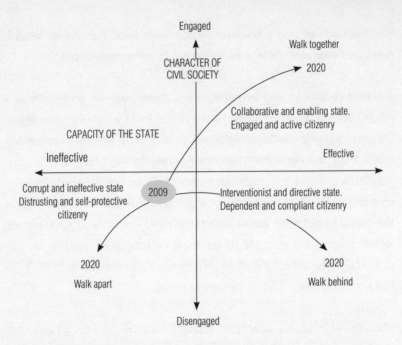

The metaphor of 'walking' suggested itself from the understanding that ours was a long journey from a discriminatory divided past towards the country of our dreams painted in our national constitution. To live the dream of a nation united in its diversity is easier said than done. The last eighteen years of living in a constitutional democracy have been marked by the tendency of citizens to leave the business of governance to government. Upwardly mobile people have tended to focus on their own advancement rather than being engaged in ensuring that the government fulfils its election promises to implement policies that will ensure an inclusive and better future for all.[73]

The 'Walk Apart' Scenario has been with us for more than a decade and a half. The 'me, myself and I' approach has not only characterised much of the attitudes of many in the business community who will stop at nothing to make a profit, but has also engulfed public servants.

The disrespectful attitudes of many teachers, nurses and other public officials whose sole focus is their own self-interest add salt to the wounds of poor people who have a legitimate expectation that the government will provide public services and assistance. In addition, corruption has reached epidemic proportions at most levels of government across the country. It is no longer a matter of a few corrupt people, but is becoming a way of governing in most spheres of government.

Njabulo Ndebele captured the current approach of the ANC and the government as 'corruptive collusion'.

> These corruptive collusions become new foundations for solidarity. They effectively replace the old solidarities of struggle. The latter, though, can continue to be invoked as a necessary mantra of commitment, and far less as an objective to be pursued. Corruptive collusions offer group protection and will be hostile towards any regulatory means whatever their merits, which emanate from outside the group. Even the National Constitution is an outside phenomenon.[74]

The government's rhetoric on corruption has lost credibility amongst citizens, more and more of whom share Ndebele's view about corruption as an entrenched political cultural feature of the ANC in power.

Passive aggression is increasingly erupting into violence and the destruction of public property. The anger of poor people is evident all over the country in so-called 'service delivery protests'. The vicious cycle of violent protests, violent police responses and more violence poses a real threat to our country's stability. The middle and upper classes are hiring more and more private security services, building higher and higher walls and relying more and more on private schools and health services. Most poor people are left with failing schools and health services and have little leverage to demand better.

The 2011 local authority elections played out a mixture of traditional loyalist voting patterns and early signs of an awareness by some voters of the power of their vote to punish underperformance by the ruling party. This nascent exercise of the power to hold government accountable may have a positive impact on the attitudes of those in power not to continue to take citizens for granted. But the majority of poor voters have again given the governing party overwhelming support overall, especially in areas such as the Eastern Cape and Limpopo Provinces. Almost immediately after the elections, the cycle of violent protests continued against the very government they had voted in.

The contradictory messages the majority of voters are sending their political representatives tell us a lot about the conflict between, on the one hand, their emotional attachment to the ANC, to which they believe they owe eternal loyalty as a liberation movement and, on the other hand, their frustration at the failure of the ANC government to fulfil its promises. This conflict lies behind the passive aggression born of powerlessness that regularly explodes into violence in which public assets are damaged or destroyed. Continuing on this pathway is likely to lead to chaos and loss of confidence in the future of the country by both citizens and investors, local and foreign, which could have devastating consequences for our economy and society.

The 'Walk Behind' Scenario is also playing out in our current reality. The 2008/9 global financial meltdown strengthened the voices of those who believe that the government should play a bigger role in the economy because the private sector had failed to act for the public good. The push for a developmental state is very strong within the ANC ranks who quote as examples the Asian Tigers of yesteryear which are strong economies today: South Korea, Singapore, Malaysia and Thailand. The reality is that a developmental state requires enormous capacity for evidence-based policy making, planning and implementation, as well as monitoring and evaluation of progress and willingness to learn from identified mistakes. In addition, the world economy has changed drastically since the heady 1970/80s era of the prowling Asian Tigers. The international trade regime makes closed economies difficult and punishes the anti-competitive protectionism that helped those Tigers to establish and enhance their manufacturing and other sectors as national champions. The competitive, interconnected and ICT driven global economy is less likely to tolerate, let alone enable, state monopolies that are unlikely to withstand competitive pressures.

Our post-1994 government has yet to demonstrate its capacity to cope with expectations of its role as an enabling state that promotes a climate for growth and development. It is puzzling that the glaring capacity gaps are being ignored in the quest for more centralised control of the economy by some sectors in the governing party. The existing State Owned Enterprises (SOEs) are struggling to become effective and efficient players in providing the key infrastructural needs of a sophisticated economy. For instance, political interference has seen the SABC weakened, Transnet is battling to keep trains moving and ports effectively providing logistical support for the booming resources sector, and Postnet is struggling to discharge its mandate due to the disabling impact of the board on the executive. Eskom is also battling the political interference that saw it running out of energy which led to the disgrace of the lights going out on South Africa in early 2007. Eskom is not yet out of the woods as it seeks to bolster funding support for long-term sustainability as competition increases from private providers in the green energy space.

It is against this background that we as citizens should be concerned about the establishment in 2010 of a State Mining Company, the African Exploration Mining & Finance Corporation (AEMFC). Where is the expertise going to come from to run this mining company in a world in which established companies are feeling the cold winds of a global shortage of mining skills? How is its performance going to be measured? How is it to be held accountable to us as citizens? Or is this going to be but one more manifestation of a push for a greater central role of government in the economy regardless of outcomes?

The clamour for nationalisation of the mines and the expropriation of land driven by the embattled president of the ANCYL, Julius Malema, is tapping into the sentiment of a developmental state. He invokes the 1955 Freedom Charter as the guiding light for his call which sends shivers down the collective spines of investors – both local and foreign. The repeated threatening posture of the leader of the ANCYL is enough to turn investor sentiment away from our country and it is creating uncertainty, notwithstanding the official government position that nationalisation is not their policy. The conflicting positions of members of the ANC on the nationalisation issue does not help, and it is hardly surprising that analysts have downgraded the country's investment status from a positive to a more negative outlook.

The trade union leadership, especially the National Union of Mine Workers (NUM), has also been ambivalent. The president was un-equivocal in distancing NUM from the call for nationalisation during an early 2011 roadshow with Minister Suzan Shabangu of the Mineral

Resources Department. He pointed to the fact that the 2002 Mineral and Petroleum Resources Development Act already vests all the mineral rights in the state which grants exploration and mining rights to companies under specified conditions, including compliance with BEE legislative and policy provisions as well as paying royalties to the state. Both the first and second drafts of the Bill provided for different royalty rates for different types of mineral. In the first draft the rates varied from zero for sands and gravel to 8 per cent for diamonds. The second draft included dual rates for certain refined and unrefined minerals, with a lower rate for refined minerals equal to half the rate for unrefined minerals. The royalty rate for diamonds in the second draft was reduced to 5 per cent.[75]

This position of the NUM has been muddied by ambiguous statements from other union officials that seem to have been driven by union leadership's fear of being perceived to be to the right of those calling for nationalisation. Positioning oneself as radical seems to be a major concern in the run-up to the 2012 ANC policy and elective conferences.

Disengaged citizens who have hitherto left matters to the government are beginning to voice concerns. The rhetoric of nationalisation is not only scaring foreign investors but local ones as well. Taxpayers are concerned about the financial implications for them as the funders of government if the nation were to assume the huge costs of expropriation. The potential cost of continuing citizen disengagement is increasing daily and the loss of jobs and livelihoods in this scenario poses a serious threat to social stability. Lessons from the Arab Spring which shook North African countries, starting with Tunisia, Egypt and Libya, need to be learnt and a change of direction charted now if we are to avoid catastrophe.

The *'Walk Together' Scenario* remains the most challenging yet the only plausible way out of the current impasse. Notwithstanding the commitment of successive post-apartheid governments to 'deliver services' to poor people, poverty remains widespread, inequality between haves and have-nots is growing, and anger and resentment are rising among the marginalised. During 2009, almost all the audiences to whom my colleagues on the Scenarios Team and I presented the scenarios, indicated a preference for 'walking together'. The most common question from all audiences was how could disengaged citizens learn to walk together after all the years of walking apart and behind?

I was quite taken aback during the dissemination of the Dinokeng Scenarios in 2009 by citizens' confession that they do not know how to walk together. Those familiar with the history of our liberation struggle would be surprised by this confession of ignorance for ours was a story of 'walking together' for freedom by various parties of the liberation movement, trade unions, religious leaders and their folk, young people at school and in higher education, as well as ordinary communities across the length and breadth of our land. Making South Africa ungovernable could not have happened without the collective effort of those not represented in government at the time together with those white people who were opposed to continuing white domination. At that time solidarity across race, class and gender faultlines was visible and palpable in a true 'walk together' for freedom. How could we have forgotten so soon after 1994?

The reality is that as citizens we acquiesced to the rewriting of the history of our struggle to make it appear as though we were liberated through the sole efforts of the ANC. There are even people who were not yet in their teens when we attained our freedom threatening voters with 'taking

Conversations with My Sons and Daughters

away the freedom we gave you' if they do not show enough gratitude to those in power. The myth that South Africans were passive recipients of freedom from a liberation movement has disempowered many into believing that they owe their freedom and future prosperity to the ANC as a liberation party, regardless of its current or future performance as a political party. The citizenship rights and responsibilities of South Africans are undermined by this myth which perpetuates the subject status of citizens which is the antithesis of freedom.

The hallmark of the 'subject' identity is lack or loss of the agency impulse which is at the heart of being human. International studies have shown that 'dominance hierarchies' focused on self-advancement and competition for status undermine the self-worth of those pushed to the bottom of such societies.[76] The growing inequalities in our society, with the Gini coefficient standing at 0.7 today, coupled with ostentatious consumption and flaunting of wealth by politically connected people, has been highly damaging to poor people. The rhetoric of *Ubuntu* without evidence of the affiliative strategies of mutuality, reciprocity, and capacity for empathy and emotional bonding with those at the bottom of the social ladder, only serves to confirm to poor people that there is something wrong with them. Many internalise the myth that their poverty is of their own making and reflects their worthlessness to society. Learning anew to 'walk together' entails embarking on a journey of healing the wounds of the past that perpetuate the disempowering social relations that characterise our society today.

The truth and reconciliation process in South Africa in the mid-1990s was a resounding success in dealing with gross violations of human rights when we dug deep within ourselves to confront and ritualise the beginnings of a healing journey for both ourselves and our country.

Many South Africans – black and white – poured out their pain in order to heal the nation and build bridges towards a better future. We should always be grateful to those who bared their souls at the TRC as well as to the ritual masters and mistresses who presided over the healing process.

It is unfortunate that the TRC process was deliberately designed to exclude all but gross violations of human rights. The political logic was understandable: compromise that involved letting go of retribution for socio-economic injustices was essential for a political settlement to be reached with the apartheid government of the day. But the importance of re-establishing the broken chain of human connectedness in the post-apartheid period was seriously underestimated. South Africa missed the opportunity to ritualise acknowledgement of our ruptured society as a foundation for starting a deeper healing process.

Non-attention to the personal humiliation, shame, loss of dignity and self-worth that was visited upon the indigenous people of this country has cost us dearly. Those defined as 'non-whites' were left to bear the psychological and socio-economic costs of violations of human rights. Public policies that established discriminatory socio-economic and political systems inflicted this pain on the majority population, while at the same time creating significant opportunities and material gains for the minority population. The irony of the situation is that the pain inflicted by public policies has been left to individuals to resolve privately without any effective assistance from society. Failure to address the impact of violations of socio-economic rights in the transition to democracy has effectively privatised the healing of social pain in South Africa.

In his later years Carl Jung wrestled with questions pertaining to what it means to be human. In his exploration of the links between human consciousness, the unconscious and something larger than humanity itself, Jung asks:

> Is a person connected with something that is infinite or not? That is the telling question of his life. In our relationships to other men too, the crucial question is whether an element of boundlessness is expressed in the relationship.[77]

Jung was struggling to understand the relationships between human beings on one hand, and those between human beings and an unknown and infinite other. At the same time he was exploring how humans are interconnected both in the present and after-life. Jung's quest led him to conclude that 'respect for the eternal rights of man, recognition of the ancient, and the continuity of culture and intellectual history' were essential to understanding who we are and where we fit in the wider scheme of the universe. He asserted that the loss of the connection with the past has given rise to the flurry to live more in the future than the present. Jung refers to this loss as 'our uprootedness'. Our roots as human beings, including our evolutionary paths, are programmed into our genes. We express not only physical and emotional characteristics that tap into our ancestral roots, but also ways of knowing that are at times inexplicable. Ignoring these ways of knowing puts people at risk of feeling uprooted – people without firm foundations.

Modern psychologists are becoming increasingly aware that 'human beings are wired for inter-connectedness'. Some authors go so far as to suggest that social connectedness is a need as basic as that for air, water, or food. The lack of a sense of social connectedness may result in deprivation that is expressed as social pain, which is to be understood as suffering caused by harm or threat to social connectedness. It is a form of emotional or psychological pain. Bereavement, embarrassment, shame and other hurt feelings are types of social pain. People who have or are suffering from social pain tend also to suffer from low self-esteem which sets off a vicious cycle of not being sociable or fun to be with. Affected individuals are often seen as brooding, undesirable social partners[78] which compounds the sense of being marginalised and excluded.

Studies have shown that people afflicted with social pain suffer depressive states manifested by apathy, suicidal feelings, helplessness and hopelessness. Self-esteem can be a measure of the extent to which one feels either included or excluded in society. The greater the sense of one's humanity being affirmed by others, the higher one's sense of worth and self-esteem will be, and such affirmation is at the heart of the well-being of human beings who are creatures meant to live in community.

More and more studies suggest that psychological or social pain has a greater impact on the sufferer than physical pain. As John Steinbeck put it in *Travels with Charley*, 'A sad soul can kill you quicker than a germ.'[79] The higher impact of social pain is accentuated by its unique ability to be re-enacted over and over again – the equivalent of reliving a nightmare. Our social legacy of exclusion and discrimination under both colonial conquest and apartheid has resulted in large sections of our society suffering from social pain. Both oppressor and oppressed are affected by abnormal social interactions occasioned by treating and being treated in a manner that breaks the chain of human connectedness.

White people have also been wounded by the pain they have inflicted on their fellow human beings. As a Native American Chief so aptly said, 'We are part of the same thread – any damage to part of the thread affects us all.' Human connectedness is such that when one of us is abused, we will feel the pain. We may deny this, but it will catch up with us sooner or later. We may dull the pain through substance abuse or putting as much distance as possible between us and the abused, but we cannot erase the impact of social pain – part of us will always hurt and be crying out for healing.

The process of healing starts with acknowledgement of the need for it, but for many the level of woundedness is so deep that they need to be supported in order to acknowledge their pain. Strong and effective leadership is essential to encourage a movement towards the quest for healing and the establishment of the TRC demonstrated our ability to learn from others, such as post-Pinochet Chile, to create a process rooted in our cultural heritage and our own political context, although we may draw on lessons from elsewhere.

What are the lessons from elsewhere in the world that we can learn from? Nicaragua is a good place to look for inspiration. The country suffered a gruelling civil war aided and abetted by the USA, ultimately reaching a settlement in the 1980s. Then the country was hit by Hurricane Mitch in 1998. Martha Cabrera, a native Nicaraguan who studied psychology and lived in the USA, shares the lessons learnt in working with a society suffering from multiple wounds five years after Hurricane Mitch. She characterised her work as 'affective and spiritual reconstruction'. She has this to say: 'Trauma and pain afflict not only individuals. When they become widespread and ongoing, they affect entire communities and even the country as a whole.' As this socially conscious psychologist explains, the implications are serious for people's health, the resilience of the country's social fabric, the success of development schemes, and the hopes of future generations.

One of the questions we asked ourselves back then, and are still asking, is what has happened to the millions invested in training in Nicaragua and what good has it left behind, because there isn't a community in this country that hasn't received a workshop on something. Everybody has been 'workshopped'. There have been workshops on gender, on environment, on civic participation, to name just a few. All the realities, not to mention all the vogues that international cooperation suggests and at times imposes have been topics of workshops all over the country. But with so much effort put into so many workshops and seminars, why were the results so poor? Why, despite so much training, were people not responding to the seriousness of the problems? Why weren't they mobilizing and making demands?

When one has a lot of accumulated pain, one loses the capacity to communicate with others. The ability to communicate, to be flexible and tolerant is enormously reduced among people who have a number of unresolved personal traumas. The characteristics vital to a person's ability to function adequately become affected. The loss of solidarity that we lament in today's Nicaragua has to do with loss of trust between people. An incredible amount of money has been spent in this country on programs to build and strengthen institutional capacity, not just in state institutions but also in non-governmental and local grassroots organizations. But the strengthening of an institution is based on mutual trust and that is one of the things that's lost when there is an accumulation of pain and misplaced intolerance and inflexibility.

Our work has obliged us to study emotions in depth. When one is sad, it's not something that affects an ear or a foot; it runs through the whole body. Emotion is energy in motion. That's why fury can make the entire body go rigid. The emotions resulting from being wounded, from trauma, which are rage, sadness, fear and guilt, automatically generate bodily changes. The body is wise and uses these changes to invite us to express the emotion. Emotion is a sign that we're alive. When we feel sad about having lost something or someone, that sadness is a sign of life. When people acknowledge pain, sadness or some other profound emotion, they usually give themselves the time needed to digest it, and when they express and reflect on it, the emotion continues its normal course, eventually dissipating. But when that acknowledgement is blocked for whatever reason, the emotions – which have an impact on the immune system, the neurological system, the circulatory system, the whole body – trigger physiological changes in blood pressure, temperature, digestion, and end up making us ill. There's always a tight relationship between the illnesses we suffer and the emotions we repress.[80]

It is sometimes difficult to explain why South Africa should be so focused on social pain from the legacy of the past, given that other post-colonial African countries have also suffered discrimination and oppression. My own view is that most Africans in post-colonial Africa *are* also affected by social pain but the difference between South Africa and the rest of the continent is the extent and impact of social pain. The visibility of the stark differences between lives of grinding poverty and those spent in comfort and conspicuous consumption rubs salt in the wounds of those enduring social pain. Given its advanced urbanised economy relative to the rest of the continent, South Africa has created intimate proximity between the haves and the have-nots in which domestic and other menial workers are daily witnesses to, and servants of, the lives of the wealthy.

Black South Africans have always been essential to the creation, maintenance and prosperity of the privileged lifestyles of their white compatriots. They have always been part of the intimate domain of homes, hospitals and retirement facilities where they have rendered essential services. They were constantly subjected to the humiliation of being denied the dignity of sharing entrances, utensils, and other basic facilities with their fellow citizens. For example, simple issues such as a clean flushing toilet for white people versus a smelly long-drop for black people working in the same company or household form part of the painful memories of many. Or black mine workers having to live in an overcrowded mine hostel whilst their white colleagues enjoy family homes. It is the relative deprivation in South Africa that makes inequality so painful for so many and the social pain so deep and so widespread in our society.

Sadly, the situation for the majority of poor black people has not changed much despite significant resources being devoted to effect change in their lives. The approach to reconstruction and development has been a top-down one that treats poor people as objects of charity or subjects, rather than fellow citizens who have the capacity for participating in the planning and implementation of programmes addressing their development needs. The perpetuation of apartheid's geography that locates poor people far from city amenities, compounded by the undignified RDP housing development, is an affront to whatever dignity poor people have managed to retain. The effect is to create a dependency syndrome which promotes further humiliation and helplessness and the poor continue to suffer social marginality in our post-apartheid society.

Look around you and ask yourself whether some of the inexplicably horrifying criminal and abusive behavioural patterns in our society are not suggestive of a people who are deeply wounded. Some of the most gruesome crimes are committed by those who feel that society has let them down and they owe it nothing. Reverence for life has gone out the window. The more worthless individuals feel, the less they value their own and other people's lives. One could also point to the destructive lifestyles of many of our young people as evidence of seriously dysfunctional families and communities. How do we explain the level of substance abuse from very young ages? How do we explain the smoking of concoctions including ARVs/dagga/rat poison/battery acid called *Nyaupe*? What about those who sell these poisons to frustrated young people? Are they not actually knowingly killing them? Many of those dealing in these concoctions are also feeding a new crime – the theft of ARVs from poor HIV positive patients whose lives are put at risk. Is ours not becoming a murderous society?

There is growing evidence of sexual activity among children as young as pre-teens. This can be partly explained by the lack of privacy in cramped houses which exposes them to their parents' sexual encounters. Many are initiated into sexual activity by older relatives or their teachers, who have multiple sexual relationships with their own pupils. This inappropriate behaviour by those in charge of guiding the development of children leads to the breakdown of moral codes of behaviour. Children are increasingly regarding having sex as minors as entertainment, as was disturbingly demonstrated by the 2010 case where two fourteen-year-old boys had sex with a fifteen-year-old girl on the Jules High School grounds in Gauteng in full view of their peers. Some of the schoolchildren recorded this horror story on their cellphones.

Our criminal justice system was found wanting in the face of this outrage. Ironically, the children were charged with violation of the law against having sex with minors! We as a society are the people who should have been charged for failing to bring up children to respect their bodies. The Education System also has to acknowledge responsibility for failing to create positive learning and teaching environments in our schools which would surely make such occurrences less likely. It is evident that idle hands and minds are a breeding ground for inappropriate behaviour in our failing school system, and the epidemic of teenage pregnancy and the continuing new HIV/AIDS infections are indicators of risk-taking that borders on suicidal behaviour.

The 2011 Human Sciences Research Council Report indicates shocking statistics of girls as young as ten years falling pregnant and testing HIV positive. HIV prevalence in the 10 to 14 year age group grew alarmingly between 2008 and 2010 from 7.3 per cent in 2008 to 7.9 per cent in 2009 and 9.1 per cent in 2010. These are young women who have unprotected sex with older men in exchange for financial and other support – the so-called 'sugar daddy' phenomenon. That an adult man can have sex with such a young child (a criminal act in South African law) is a reflection of the level of moral decay in our society and the willingness of young girls to experiment with sex at such young ages reflects the failure of our society to nurture and protect its young.

The cost of the neglect of social pain is everywhere in evidence. How else does one explain the fact that after more than eighteen years of freedom the majority of South African pupils are being denied opportunities to forge successful careers of their choosing because of a failing Education System, despite Education as a sector enjoying the highest allocation of government expenditure? How do we explain the low levels of expectation of the capacity of pupils and teachers to create high quality teaching and learning outcomes? Sadly, South Africa today not only underperforms in comparison with poor countries such as Lesotho, Swaziland and Malawi, but in many ways education outcomes are worse than those under apartheid.

It would appear that there are many self-destructive patterns of behaviour in our society that point to a lack of self-respect as a nation which has no ambition to achieve excellence.

This is reflected in our lack of civic pride. Take the city of Johannesburg. Why does it have to be so filthy that one can hardly recognise the Eloff Street that used to be its pride? Why has the parking garage near Park Station become a dumping site in full view of anyone entering the city from Braamfontein, including the mayor of the metropolis? Pavements and streets are in an advanced state of disrepair in the heart of the city that is the financial capital of our country. A block away from the ABSA Bank downtown headquarters is a street mechanic's workshop creating an unsightly mess on the pavement without anyone calling the offender to book. Pavements are congested with garbage and the merchandise of informal traders, but neither rules nor urban by-laws are enforced. Why is there such tolerance for irresponsible use of public spaces?

Visit any public institution or public space and you will see how little pride people have in their environment. By and large, our cities are unkempt. Our hospitals are a disgrace and an affront to the dignity of the patients who are forced to use them as well as the health personnel who are employed there. One such health facility in a rural area of our beloved country was so dreadful that I pleaded with the nurses working there not ever to let expectant mothers give birth in the dusty 'labour ward' with its leaking roof. One could just see postnatal sepsis waiting for any woman unfortunate enough to give birth there. The facility was once used as a shebeen but it was converted into a 'health centre' by the Eastern Cape post-apartheid government without any thought being given to the importance of hygiene and human dignity. Is it any surprise that maternal mortality rates have quadrupled since 1994 and infant mortality rates are rising despite our commitment to the Millennium Development Goals to reduce these rates?

If you use our road network you literally take your life into your own hands. Countless lives are lost every day because of reckless driving and a disregard for the rules of the road that defies imagination. Double barrier lines, blind rises and curves are no impediment to impatient overtaking especially by drivers of trucks and minibus taxis. One also has to contend with unroadworthy vehicles that put other motorists at risk. Drag racing has become a favoured sport, often claiming innocent lives, including those of the schoolchildren who were mown down in Soweto in 2010 by a socialite named Jub Jub and his friend. Drinking and driving is as rife as ever. There seems to be no end to the suicidal activities of our wounded nation.

The law seems to be dead on many fronts and many are losing their lives in the process. Our law enforcement system is unable to rise to the challenge of controlling unlawful behaviour. The men and women in uniform are themselves wounded as evidenced by the epidemic of overweight and, in some cases, gross obesity amongst our officers. Despite the intervention of the former Commissioner of Police, Bheki Cele, many police officers are simply unfit for the tough duty of chasing criminals. There is the sense that many seek comfort for their woundedness in food, while others engage in corruption out of a sense of entitlement to reward for their services, or by turning a blind eye in exchange for money or other favours.

We have also witnessed a return to apartheid style policing. The safety and security service system of law enforcement, tempered by respect for human rights, has been replaced by a police force approach. The cry from the leadership is 'shoot to kill'. Reports of police brutality are a growing reality and the number of deaths in police custody bring back painful memories of deaths in detention during the apartheid era.

Institute of Security Studies figures show that over the last three years deaths from police shootings have doubled from 281 in 2005/2006 to 521 in 2010. Overall deaths in police custody or resulting from police action rose to 860 in 2009/2010 from 695 in the five-year period 2003/2008. South Africa has the highest recorded rates of homicides by police officers in the world. The USA, with a population of 311 million, had 439 arrest-related homicides by law enforcement officers in 2006. In 2010 England and Wales, with a combined population of 54 million had just one fatal shooting in police custody – a stark contrast to our 521 in a population of 49 million.[81]

A recent graphic illustration of the brutality of our police was the killing of a defenceless protester in Ficksburg on 21 April 2011. Andries Tatane, a leader in a poor community in the town, died after being attacked by police with batons and rubber bullets in full view of television cameras. This incident closely mirrors the 1991 Los Angeles Police Department murder of Rodney King that led to widespread riots in the city and the eventual resignation of Daryl Gates, the police chief at the time. Just as Daryl Gates sought to dismiss the incident as the work of 'bad apples', so too Bheki Cele, then Police Commissioner, wanted us to believe that in a police force of 190 000 'some kids are bound to step out of line'.[82]

The reality is that the sharp increase in the police's violent actions against citizens is related to the institutional culture that is being fostered in the service. The Zuma government decided in 2010 to return us to the era of military titles and a hierarchical system. The leadership approach of the generals, lieutenants and captains reinforces the military culture with force and might as the desirable style. Instead of seeking to understand the root causes of crime and insecurity in our society, the police focus on displaying their ability to meet fire with fire. Whilst this might work against some hard-core criminals, it is an inappropriate approach to crime prevention and the promotion of secure communities. The majority of our criminals are from the 3 to 4 million 18 to 35-year-olds who have been failed by our education and training system and the jobless economic growth pattern of the past decade and a half. They are wounded young (and not so young) people who have given up on their society ever providing them with a future in which they can prosper. Shooting them as 'bastards', as the then Deputy Minister of Police Suzan Shabangu said on 10 August 2008, will simply harden their criminal resolve.

The militarisation of the police is being actively cultivated in the training programmes that subject young recruits to brutality. Many of these recruits are wounded people who join the police service out of desperation to find a pathway out of prolonged unemployment and poor quality education and training outcomes. Their self-esteem is low and their trust in their fellow citizens is compromised by life on the margins of a highly unequal society. Trainees report being shouted at, slapped and subjected to extreme physical exercise in order to 'toughen them'. They themselves understand that 'when you are punished all the time you become aggressive. The instructors call us shovels and say shovels don't get tired. They also say "comply and complain later". Even when you know an instructor is wrong, you just follow instructions.'[83]

Experience all over the world is that violence begets violence. Reimposing apartheid style police brutality is simply going to escalate the woundedness in our society. Our departure from a human rights based law enforcement approach to one of brutality is bound to worsen the level of crime and the depths of its brutality. The 'macho' approach by police in a society riddled with wounded male egos is bound to backfire and lead us into becoming an even more violent and crime-ridden society.

I would like to propose that your generation pays more attention to how our legacy and the social pain it has caused are impacting on our social relationships. We need to ask how much social pain may have affected our ability as a society to live out the *Ubuntu* ideals that as South Africans we are rightly proud of. Has the exclusion of, and discrimination against, the majority population made us much more determined to cherish and live out *Ubuntu* or not? How much social pain are we inadvertently continuing to inflict on those who remain excluded from opportunities while we repeatedly affirm our adherence to *Ubuntu*? Are we not adding insult to injury in being seen as hypocritical by sustaining such a large discrepancy between our rhetoric and the reality of our relationships with one another?

How much pain are we inflicting as a society by the continuing inequalities of opportunity in our public and private lives despite the precepts of our human rights based constitution? To what extent has the social pain of being excluded from key opportunities for self-actualisation been internalised by the majority of the population? To what extent is social pain behind some of the disappointing behaviours of fellow citizens in homes, communities, workplaces and wider public life? And what about your own personal lives?

I would like to suggest that the failure to acknowledge and undertake the healing process to address social pain is at the heart of our failure to make the journey from subjects to citizens. In his seminal work, Mahmood Mamdani[84] analysed the difference between subject and citizen and reached the conclusion that Africa has still to develop a stronger foundation for citizenship. Mamdani demonstrates how post-colonial Africa has succeeded in only the first of the three elements necessary to decolonise the continent: deracialisation, detribalisation and democratisation. Whilst I agree that deracialisation is the only area of success, I would argue that even that success is superficial in most cases and is easily reversed as political leaders reach for the race card in order to cling to power, as Robert Mugabe has so effectively demonstrated in Zimbabwe.

The failure to detribalise reflects the complex legacy of divide and rule that creates vested interests in maintaining traditional leadership structures as part of the patronage system. President Nyerere of Tanzania imposed a top-down detribalisation process in Tanzania which bought the country time to wean the population from dependence on ethnicity as a political tool. The insistence by Nyerere that all Tanzanians learn to write and speak KiSwahili went a long way to creating a national identity uncluttered by ethnic affiliations so often reflected in language usage. Nyerere is perhaps the only African leader who actively educated his countrymen for national identity beyond the tribe.

South Africa has opted to reinforce tribalism by perpetuating the imposition of traditional leaders on rural people and thus condemning them to remain subjects. The rights of rural citizens are compromised by this dual allegiance to the state with its human rights national constitution that entitles them to equality before the law, yet also forces them to pay homage as subjects of an inherited leadership system. The situation of women and children is even worse for the right to gender equality and the rights of the child are subordinated to traditional customs. How can such citizens become active agents of their own development? Maintaining the subject status of rural people is a political convenience for the ANC as the governing party because rural voters are often compelled to follow the direction of their traditional leaders in making political choices. Such coercion is also not uncommon in a system that rewards loyalty with generous patronage. Given how many traditional leaders are benefiting from the status quo, it is not surprising that there is no political will to transform rural social relations.

The process of democratisation requires commitment by citizens and leaders alike to embark on a journey to unlearn the authoritarian culture of the past which still permeates our homes, our schools, our workplaces and some civil society structures such as trade unions and churches. It is my view that the transformation of our identities from those of subjects to citizens requires a commitment to the journey of healing.

CHAPTER 8

EXPERIMENTS IN ADDRESSING SOCIAL PAIN

The world is beginning to understand the importance of not only acknowledging social pain but of addressing it in a culturally appropriate way for each context. What is no longer in dispute is that social pain is a major determinant of ill-health and an obstacle to sustainable development.

The traditional approach to human needs framed by Maslow's Hierarchy of Needs that sets basic biological needs above psycho-social ones is being questioned by emerging studies of human behaviour. The idea that biological and safety needs have to be met before needs of belongingness and love, esteem and self-actualisation stands challenged by growing evidence that failure to meet higher order needs makes meeting basic needs unsustainable. The need to belong is basic for all human beings; it is what makes us human. Let us look at a few examples.

Nicaragua was fortunate to have one of its own, native psychologist Martha Cabrera, to undertake addressing the social pain she had identified, as described in Chapter 7.[85] Cabrera and her team focused on the question: 'How does one empower a traumatised population?' She recounts how municipal mayors and government departments were perplexed as to why people often didn't want to participate in their own development schemes, such as rebuilding their own houses. The sentiment is often put forward that people don't want to change, aren't interested in their development. Why should this be?

Martha Cabrera uses a simple metaphor:

> When people are hit by a car on the street, they don't just get up, brush off the gravel, go on to work and forget about it. The very least they will do is to tell others about what happened, get it off their chest, tend their wounds. Well, Nicaragua hasn't just been hit by a car; it has been run over by a long train!

The journey of healing, then, starts with personal stories, personal histories which become 'a river of life'. These personal histories go into rewriting the national history – personal rivers of life flowing into the nation's river of life. Textbooks had to be rewritten to enable people to process the pain, see their history through different eyes and move beyond it. The personal and national are intertwined and it is difficult to build a democracy when a country's personal history still hurts.

It was also found that organisational models and leadership styles are shaped by the extent to which social pain has been dealt with or not. Cabrera's team introduces four modules:

1. Personal Sphere – crises, wounds, health, the conception of healing, lifestyle and holistic health habits
2. Historical-cultural Sphere – how our personal life is marked by the country's history and the national culture, how many dysfunctional strategies our culture has and how they are expressed
3. What organisational form we establish
4. Development model that acknowledges and promotes healing of social pain

Nicaragua's experience emphasises the importance of collective healing rituals that promote the unity of mind, soul and body. Cabrera asserts that:

> Multiply wounded societies run the risk of becoming societies with inter-generational traumas. It is virtually a law that one treats others the way one treats oneself. Anywhere that large population groups are traumatized, the trauma is transferred to the next generation.

In essence, the process of healing is about assuming personal responsibility, distancing oneself from traditional ways of doing things, and learning new ways of being whole as persons, as leaders and as citizens.

Similar work is being done amongst First Nations People in Canada. This issue was thrust to the fore by the high levels of dysfunctional families and substance abuse despite efforts to address these social ills.

Something deeper needed to be engaged to enable communities that were living in the twilight to emerge and assume their citizenship roles.

In 1996 a final report of the Royal Commission on Aboriginal Peoples (RCAP) recognised that the future must include the opportunity for former students of residential schools to share their stories to help shed light on a significant part of Canadian history.[86] The wounds of abused students, the denigration of their culture and forced assimilation into European culture would not heal without a systematic telling of the stories of what happened. The report led to the setting up of the Aboriginal Healing Foundation in 1998 to support healing initiatives for Métis, Inuit and First Nations People. A dispute resolution mechanism was agreed upon which provided a fair process to hear all claims of abuse and to verify them with a view to a holistic, fair and just settlement. This led to the largest class action settlement in Canadian history – $2 billion including the following measures:

- Common Experience Payment to be paid to all eligible former students
- Independent Assessment Process for claims of sexual and serious physical abuse
- Truth and Reconciliation Commission
- Commemorative Activities
- Measures to support healing such as the Indian Residential Schools Resolution Health Support Programme and an endowment to the Aboriginal Healing Foundation

As of 1 July 2009, the TRC chaired by Justice Murray Sinclair and two other commissioners started their five-year mandate aimed at:

- Preparing a comprehensive historical record of the policies and operations of the schools
- Completing a full and accessible report with recommendations to the government
- Establishing a research centre as a permanent resource for all Canadians
- Hosting of national events to promote awareness and public education about the history of these schools and its impact
- Support Community Initiatives to meet their unique needs and heal their wounds
- Support Commemoration Initiative to honour and affirm former students

The Canadian experience has borrowed from our own TRC process, but focused and expanded it to deal with socio-economic and psychological wounds, which we avoided doing. There are some lessons here for us as we wrestle with the ongoing bleeding of wounds in our nation that has yet to call itself by its own name – South African. We also failed to follow through with some of the minimalist recommendations of our TRC because our government attached little importance to the actions to be taken and the impact such actions could have on the lives and well-being of ordinary citizens. This failure has hurt poor women, represented most visibly by the Khulumani (speak up) NGO, which mobilised women to be witnesses at the TRC. Their stories and their willingness to forgive perpetrators of human rights abuses contributed significantly to the success of the TRC. But they remain in limbo to date.

What can we do now?

Letsema Circle, a social enterprise founded by the author, has been experimenting with how one can heal wounded people in South Africa and enable them to become engaged citizens. There are interesting similarities between our post-apartheid experiences and those of Nicaragua and, in some respects, the Canadian First Nations People. We, too, are multiply wounded people as manifested by our underperformance as a nation relative to our potential.

What is the Letsema Circle Healing approach?

The Letsema Healing Circle approach starts with an understanding that before you can walk together as a people you need to sit down and talk. Such talks start with how we sit together. The African traditional dialogue platform is the circle. It constitutes a level playing field that includes everybody and places everyone on the same plane making eye contact possible. Circles also allow growth without disrupting form – one simply makes the circle bigger to embrace newcomers or additional entrants. We deliberately evoke the traditional custom of calling an *Ilima* or *letsema* – a collective action forum – to address problems that are too big for individuals to deal with on their own.

In evoking African cultural idioms we are heeding Carl Jung's injunction to acknowledge that our heritage from previous generations is not only genetic, but includes the important element of cultural heritage that helps us to be a rooted people. By leveraging Africa's strong cultural heritage we are able to draw everyone into closer encounters on a level playing field. Communities are also drawn by the use of familiar metaphors, indigenous language and the rapport that is almost instantaneous among total strangers. Our circles of healing are affirmative spaces for communities that are often looked down upon and suffer from an inferiority complex. Affirming their cultural practices, language and idioms is an essential step in the revival of *Ubuntu* – 'I am because you are'.

Module 1: Dialogues start with acknowledgement of the presence of others. The isiZulu greeting captures it best: '*Sawubona*', literally, 'we are seeing you'. Being seen and acknowledged is an affirmation of being connected with those around one and thereby be affirmed as part of the human family. *Ubuntu* is captured as that moment of recognition and being seen – that you are affirmed as a human being through recognition of your humanity by other human beings. The Jungian question in Chapter 7 of our boundlessness as human beings is answered by our extension into the being of our fellow humans within and across generations.

The greeting allows one to feel connected enough to introduce oneself, not just by the name and surname, but also the clan name. Clans are sub-groups within ethnic entities, but also cross group entities that link people together across boundaries. Clan names such as *Dlamini, Chezi, Tolo, Mamkwena, Xhamela, Mira* often reveal interrelationships within a given dialogue circle. Individuals within these circles sharing clan names immediately feel drawn to others with whom they are connected by virtue of marriage or other relationships. These interconnections further strengthen the sense of belonging that is critical to finding common purpose.

Letsema Circle creates circles of encounters that permit these connect-ions to be discovered and acknowledged from the first entry point into a new area as depicted below:

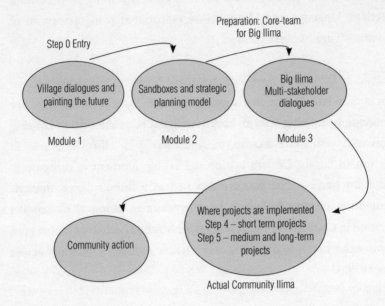

Just like the people of Nicaragua, South Africans need to tell their personal, community and national stories about how we came to where we are sitting in the circle. The myths that have been perpetuated to serve the interests of those seeking to dominate others by rewriting history need to be challenged by the rewritten personal histories that tell a different narrative. The personal stories of those around the circle tell of successes, failures, joys and disappointments. When sorrow overcomes storytellers, songs are interjected to lighten the moment. The personal stories are then woven into a picture depicting how life is experienced by those sitting in the circle and the root causes of the challenges that are at the centre of their concerns.

An important element of Module 1 is to allow a 10 to 15-minute silence for participants to take a deep breath, relax and imagine a world without the challenges they have shared. What would their personal lives look like? What kind of community would theirs be? What sounds would they hear? What smells would they encounter? What conversations would they hear? What songs would mark their daily encounters? The moment of silence creates an 'imagined space' that many at the edge of survival do not have the luxury to experience.

For many participants this period of silence is a challenging moment. Many may not ever have had the experience of sitting in silence in a group of people. We tend to be uncomfortable with silence and are often quick to fill it with words, even meaningless words. We have found that just leaving the silence to be there – uninterrupted – is transformational. It enables people to have the space to imagine without the clutter of other people's voices. This 'imagined space' is both daunting and liberating for people living in overcrowded noisy spaces for out of it emerge dreams that lift people beyond the daily grind of poverty and indignity.

The next step in the module is for the participants to express their dreams in paintings on a large white sheet of paper shared with four to six other participants. For many it is the first time that they will hold a paint brush or a writing implement but initial reticence gives way to enthusiastic brightly coloured images of envisaged futures. The child in the participant is awakened to render wonderful images of dreams deferred by years of disappointments. Participants then share their dreams around the table and identify shared dreams and each table takes turns to explain to others around the room what their table's dreams are as depicted on each canvas. The similarities of the dreams is often striking even though the symbols used to depict them may differ.

The final step is further dialogue about how one turns dreams into reality in a given community. Assets that each participant brings to the table to address the challenges listed by all are identified: skills sets, knowledge of different types, including indigenous knowledge of flora and fauna, land or other physical assets and so on. This asset-based approach is a major step in transformative development approaches in contrast to a deficit-focused one. The question is not 'What can I do for you?' or 'What can the government do for you?' but 'What are the assets you bring to the table to contribute to a shared development effort?' The assumption that poor people have no assets is what is so disempowering to so many people in our society. The dignity of being recognised as a value-adder, rather than as a person with deficiencies who is the subject of hand-outs, enables greater capacity to contribute more and own the success of whatever is co-created.

Identification of what can be done within the community in the short term without outside help is an essential building block for enhancing mastery within poor communities. It awakens in them their capabilities to tackle problems without having to wait for outside intervention. For example, in one of the clinics in the Eastern Cape, volunteers from local villages begged the local Spar for vegetables that were getting close to their 'sell by date' so they could make soup for poor people who came hungry to the clinic to collect their ARVs. It took these villagers one session of Module 1 during early 2011 to realise that in fact they should be growing their own vegetables around the clinic building. The fertile land was buried under unsightly weeds which had been left to thrive because the community regarded the clinic as government property and in their view the government should do the weeding! The clinic now has a thriving vegetable garden from which they are able to harvest surplus vegetables to sell to the same local Spar. In addition, people have gone back to having vegetable gardens around their own homes year-round with noticeable improvement in their nutritional status.

Module 1 includes identification of what can be dealt with in the medium term by mobilising more resources from outside those of the immediate community, such as churches, schools, and other community-based organisations. We have discovered many community-based organisations, the majority of which are faith-based and committed to their communities. The fragmentation of effort was identified as the enemy of progress in many communities. The Ilima process is also beginning to promote collective action between community-based groups for greater success. Long-term efforts that will require larger outside resources from government and the private sector are identified and deferred to the next stage without allowing them to undermine internal community efforts.

Module 2 focuses on how the participants in an Ilima can turn their dreams into reality over a five-year horizon – a strategic plan on sand. Using a sand box, participants model what needs to be done in years one, two, three, four and five in a manner that anticipates bottlenecks and identifies and manages risks. Playing with sand and building clay models to symbolise buildings and livestock, and using sticks and other trinkets to model community development over a five-year period releases enormous creative energy in people who have never been challenged to model anything. The freedom to play with sand and to model a strategic plan is exhilarating for many participants and initial self-doubt gives way to growing self-confidence as they test their capacities to create new possibilities.

Mistrust of others, which often reflects lack of trust in oneself, gives way to greater trust as they play and work together in a non-threatening environment. For example, in the Duncan Village[87] Ilima in late 2010, participants demonstrated an amazing capacity to model systematic slum clearance with meticulous attention to detail and sequencing. The first year focused on moving residents of two blocks of shacks off the land to a temporary facility on local school grounds to allow the laying of infrastucture and preparation of the land for building homes. They also understood the need for a street committee system to maintain order, prevent land invasion and to keep the collective effort energised. They proposed multistorey apartment style social housing to increase the carrying capacity of the land. The process was to be repeated in year two with a further two blocks and so on until the job was completed.

The capacity of poor people to plan is often underestimated, but with the right environment and space they show remarkable understanding of the complexity of development challenges and the skill to identify and manage risks. It is this untapped capacity that could be harnessed to drive participatory involvement that is essential for sustainable development. The process of participation and the affirmation of the dignity of those often marginalised enhances human and social capital and creates a positive environment for further human and social capital formation. Participatory development sets off a virtuous cycle. The diagram below represents our understanding of how and why the Ilima approach works.

Circles of Healing

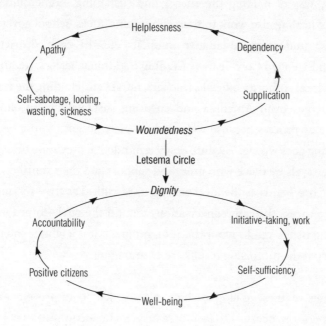

The Letsema Circle approach is turning subjects with low self-esteem, mistrust, dependency, helplessness and self-destructive lifestyles into dignified citizens. It is a slow process that needs continual reinforcement to keep those accustomed to being subjects walking together towards their citizenship entitlements and responsibilities. We like to look at the slow, gentle process as the equivalent of the South African tradition of cooking in a three-legged cast iron pot, the so-called *potjiekos*. The metaphor also captures patience, as reflected in the long, slow cooking process, and openness to unusual and experimental ingredients and the collective nature of the cooking process.

We found that establishing Core Teams in each area around a health facility and training team members to conduct circles of healing was the only way of holding the energy and sustaining momentum. The circles of healing also work to train clinic committees, school governing councils, student representative councils etc. In each district we establish Extended Core Teams including traditional healers, traditional leaders, local authority officials, teachers, nurses etc. Holding the energy that emerges from Amalima and ensuring sustainability of effort is not an easy process because wounded people will quickly lose heart if something goes wrong. They are easily reminded of previous social pain from betrayals by those who promised support and then vanished. The role of Core Teams as the local energisers is critical as they sustain the healing process through conversations around the circle to tackle any emerging issues and to report back on progress. It is a labour-intensive process but the promising results are encouraging.

Outcomes of these dialogues have already led to improvements in school performance, health facility management, identification of livelihood opportunities and support from the private sector to promote entrepreneurship. Young men and women are also being trained to use mobile technology to collect and analyse household data to set baselines for interventions within various communities. In many cases these data are the first and most reliable information gathered from poor communities who are often not counted, not even in national censuses. Importantly, the results of the surveys are fed back to communities to enable them to understand their situation better and to encourage them to change it.

Given that Letsema Circle's entry point is health system reform in line with the National Department of Health's focus on revitalising primary health care, we are placing great emphasis on identifying households with the major drivers of the high disease burden in the Eastern Cape: HIV/AIDS, TB, hypertension and diabetes. We are planning on displaying the data collected and analysed from sub-districts and larger settlements on large posters at health facilities to map trends in these major health problems. A large part of our programme is focused on enabling communities to understand the link between lifestyle and health outcome so that they can participate in the promotion of better health and the prevention of common diseases.

Our approach is also based on an understanding of the interrelationships between social circumstances and health outcomes and we therefore focus our work with communities on three areas: health system reform, education and livelihoods. The following diagram depicts how these operate – the greater the degree of overlap the more synergies emerge to enhance outcomes and sustainability.

Circles Capturing the Importance of Social Determinants of Health

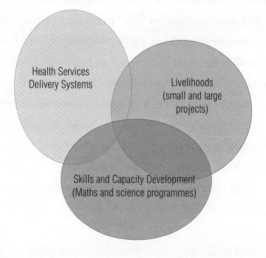

The journey from subject to citizen is an arduous one for the poor rural communities we work with. The challenges are manifold. First, change is a painful process. It involves personal commitment to let go of the crutches one has become accustomed to. It is much easier to blame others for one's own situation than to take responsibility for it oneself. Second, the process of change involves growth in areas one may find frightening. Finding and using one's voice after suffering in silence is not easy. The support networks within the circle may make it easier to find the self-confidence to speak up, but being alone at home or at work with abusive relationships is another matter. The new-found voice may falter and turn silent again. Social networks and support systems are critical to sustain change – they become the anchors of social capital development that enables greater human capital growth. The reinforcement of supportive social networks by Core Team members is essential to holding up the energy generated in Ilimas as a source of ongoing inspiration and support.

The most difficult aspect of the journey from subject to citizen is the continuing negative impact of the prevailing authoritarian social relations – at home, at work, at community level – and relationships with government at the local, provincial and national levels. The discord between the tone of conversation in healing circles and the daily realities of those who often have to go back to dysfunctional relationships has the potential to undermine progress. It is therefore critically important to promote networks of support and to move from conversations to living the dreams in projects and programmes. It is essential to move from small pilots to sub-district and district level programmes to create a self-sustaining momentum for change.

The resistance of those who have become accustomed to dealing with subjects and now have to account to citizens is not to be underestimated. We have sought to include everyone in our circles of healing: traditional leaders, traditional healers, teachers, nurses, faith-based leaders, local and provincial officials and authorities as well members of the private sector. The response has been very positive all round, although we have also experienced resistance from traditional leaders who are not yet ready to relinquish control over patronage systems that impede local development.

A classical example was the disruption of a Donor Learning Journey[88] organised in May 2011 that was intended to expose our donor partners to the sub-district areas we work in and the way we work. The journey ended in a guest house in Queenstown where we were to have a debriefing dinner for our guests. The dinner venue was invaded by rival groups of community members from two traditional areas who sought to position themselves to benefit from whatever pledges of support were to be made at the dinner. What was to have been a relaxed dinner became a tense affair until the rival factions realised that there was no money on the table except R3 million pledged by the Chris Hani Local Authority to support the use of the Ilima method to strengthen community participation in their processes to generate consensus on Integrated Development Plans (IDP). This invasion and the tensions it represented was a reminder to us that the journey is likely to be long and difficult.

The question is whether this experiment in the Eastern Cape could be adapted to other settings and, if so, how would that process unfold? The Ilima/Letsema method is a flexible process that can be modelled in appropriate ways for both rural and urban settings. The Duncan Village example above shows its applicability in an urban environment. The Buffalo City Municipality has recently requested the Letsema Team to do Ilimas in all the wards under their authority in preparation for greater participatory engagement to inform their IDPs that are traditionally drafted by consultants with little community participation. We are also working with rural development agency ASGISA to help them implement an Anti-Poverty Programme using our methodology. The challenge is going to be the willingness of new partners to change their mindsets to the participatory engaged citizen vision in implementing whatever plans are agreed to. Failure to do so will be a betrayal of those citizens who have shown commitment to the process. It is critical for Letsema Circle to walk alongside committed citizens to affirm their new-found voices to hold to account those who are betraying them.

The Letsema Circle Open Hand Approach captured below has guided us in our work in communities rich and poor

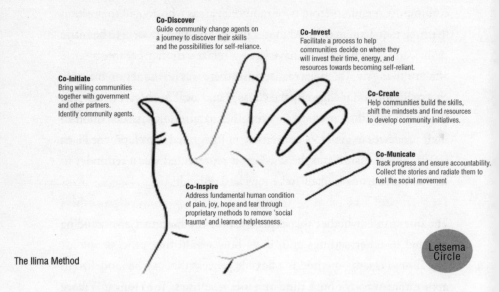

Co-Discover
Guide community change agents on a journey to discover their skills and the possibilities for self-reliance.

Co-Invest
Facilitate a process to help communities decide on where they will invest their time, energy, and resources towards becoming self-reliant.

Co-Initiate
Bring willing communities together with government and other partners. Identify community agents.

Co-Create
Help communities build the skills, shift the mindsets and find resources to develop community initiatives.

Co-Municate
Track progress and ensure accountability. Collect the stories and radiate them to fuel the social movement

Co-Inspire
Address fundamental human condition of pain, joy, hope and fear through proprietary methods to remove 'social trauma' and learned helplessness.

Letsema Circle

The Ilima Method

The 'open hand' approach invites fellow citizens into a process in which the initiation of planning must be shared by citizens, government and

Conversations with My Sons and Daughters

the private sector. Community members are often not aware of their talents and skills because they have been treated disrespectfully. Co-discovery of the assets residing in communities is a liberating process that unleashes energy for sustainable development. Communities are often keen to co-invest in development programmes but their voices are crowded out by officials and development workers and activists too keen to disburse money before assessing what exists within even the poorest communities. The opportunity to co-create new ways of doing things with communities requires time and patience because people who have lost confidence in themselves need time to regain their self-confidence. Once allowed to emerge, their creativity becomes the fuel to drive unstoppable development efforts as witnessed by many examples of illiterate people producing amazing artistic work when they are given the space to dream and represent their dreams.

We have touched on the need to sustain the energy of poor communities in a disempowering political culture. Of course, communication is vital to success and one has to find ways of connecting through media that will appeal to communities struggling on the edge of survival. Communication has to be sustained and messages must resonate with daily realities. Co-inspiration is a complementary focus to communication and is crucial when so much is dispiriting in the lives of those on the margins of society. Inspiration is also an essential factor for successful leadership; servant leaders should not only inspire others but also enable them to co-inspire their peers by sharing the joy of being an active citizen.

As we have already noted, the process of learning how to walk and work together is slow and time consuming, but the rewards are both exciting and durable. Patience is a commodity in short supply in our era of focus on timelines, meeting targets, instant messaging and pursuit of instant gratification, but participatory democracy requires meticulous attention to human interactions and the necessity for adopting a pace that can be met by the slowest in the group or team to ensure that fragile egos are affirmed and trust is built. Investing in this slow uptake pays handsome returns as self-confidence grows and creative energy is released by people normally discounted in the development process.

We have been approached to expand our work in other provinces. Our preferred approach would be to assess the state of each province, develop a map of who the existing actors are and the extent to which there are complementarities between what they are currently doing and what Letsema is doing. Identifying entry points that enhance cross-learning is a helpful way of engaging others in a non-threatening way. It is also true that Letsema Circle team members can learn a lot from others to enrich their own work and we have already found interesting opportunities in Mpumalanga and are exploring others in North West Province. The training of trainers to work in other parts of the country will be essential to ensure that we leverage local knowledge and idioms that resonate in each area to enhance acceptance by locals. We are confident that through learning by doing we can successfully leverage this methodology and apply it flexibly elsewhere.

In the spirit of Dinokeng, I would suggest that more sophisticated audiences such as you, my sons and daughters, should organise yourselves into Ten by Ten groups around dinner or lunch tables to map your own journeys from subjects to citizens. How do you understand how we have come to where we are? What are the elements that have inhibited your ability to exercise your citizenship rights and responsibilities? What would the future of your country look like if you were to start this journey together with your fellow circle members? Spend ten minutes or so in silent reflection and then share your dreams. It would be good to end on a note of what each of you would commit to doing differently as individuals, and then how as a group you will keep in touch and report back on progress. Try to touch base as the same group a month later and share experiences: what worked, what didn't, and how to do better.

I would suggest that each of you commit to approaching another ten people to form the next circle to expand conversations about the future of our country. Such conversations could become empowering encounters that will free you from the fear of the unknown which comes with any form of change. Strength in numbers often helps to overcome the fear which is common among those living as subjects. One even becomes afraid to think differently from what might be regarded as 'appropriate thoughts' because subjects don't allow themselves to entertain thoughts that those in power might construe as politically incorrect.

I have had many encounters with my peers and with yours who express fear about speaking out against what they see as going wrong in our beloved country. When asked to name what they are afraid of, most look sheepish and on reflection many say that they do not want to offend those in authority. When asked whether they regard not offending those in authority as more important than holding the same people accountable for the election promises they made and for respecting the principles of our human rights based constitution, the sheepish look returns. Some are honest enough to say that they would not want to put their businesses or careers at risk in the current political environment. Some point to examples of their colleagues' experiences of being shut out of business and career opportunities to indicate how real and high the risks are.

One cannot help but conclude that a significant proportion of South African citizens have once again become prisoners of fear. The fear that held back the march of freedom in the 1960s after the banning of liberation movements and the imprisonment of many leaders and activists has returned in an insidious manner. In the 1960s citizens were afraid of a brutal apartheid regime that stopped at nothing in order to protect white domination and privilege. Many lost loved ones and friends to relentless hit squads, deaths in detention were a regular occurrence and long-term imprisonment was the order of the day. Now, in twenty-first century democratic South Africa, the fear is largely related to loss of access to opportunities to improve one's material conditions. Being frozen out of business or career opportunities can be ruinous for those on the wrong side of political loyalties.

The question citizens have to ask themselves is how we have come to this place? How can we be afraid of the very people who are meant to represent us in government? The issue turns on our understanding of what it means to be a citizen. A citizen in a constitutional democracy is the sovereign with the power to elect and hold those in authority to account for their performance as public representatives. Citizens also have the power of the vote to dismiss those who fail to discharge their responsibilities in office. What makes us as citizens of this beautiful country so powerless and fearful?

Fear of those in authority is associated with the status of being a subject in an authoritarian system. A subject lives in fear of displeasing the master, the chief or the person seen as having authority over them. Subjects also live in fear of arbitrary acts which may involve withholding or reduction of benefits as well as the meting out of punishment; it is the arbitrariness of rewards and punishments that strike fear and terror in those treated as subjects. Could it be that as citizens of our young democracy we have yet to shed the mantle of subjects which we had to wear during apartheid? Could it be that we have retained the same relationships with those in authority as we had with the unrepresentative regimes of yesteryear? Could it be that our freedom has yet to extend to the deep psycho-social level where our self-concept and dignity reside?

In Chapter 3 we explored how the system of values embedded in our national constitution are reflected in our way of life at home, at work, in the communities we live in and the wider social arena. In particular, we returned to Frantz Fanon's concept of the importance of framing one's approach to social relationships in terms of 'being' rather than 'having'.[89] One of the features of post-apartheid South Africa is the resurgence of materialistic values amongst most sectors of society – both black and white. The over-emphasis on material goods as a mark of status is driving many citizens towards lifestyles that are barely affordable and financed largely by debt. The vulnerability that this attachment to material goods introduces in people's lives makes it difficult for many to make the kinds of choices that may put their status at risk by virtue of being shut off from opportunities for material gain.

But being dependent on material goods to define who you are as a human being goes further towards sacrificing your 'being' as a self-respecting person in order to sustain your 'having'. It seems to me that many South Africans have fallen prey to the 'having' imperative to the extent of neglecting their responsibilities to maintain their human dignity and exercise their citizenship roles. Those who have come new to wealth are particularly vulnerable given the fresh memories of poverty they still harbour. The responsibilities to extended family members loom large for first generation middle and upper-class people for whom the burden of high expectations of support from relatives can be overwhelming. It is easy to rationalise one's passivity as being in the interests of the many dependants one is responsible for. How long can one sustain such onerous responsibilities at the cost of disengaging from responsibilities as citizens? Would it not be better to ensure that your relatives benefit as they should from social services they are entitled to than to act as a source of unsustainable charity? Experience worldwide points to the reality that citizens get the governments they deserve. So the choice is ours.

The majority of South Africans who have the advantage of old money have often opted for the easy route of being free-riders in both the old and the new era of our political system. Many are cynical of the political process as a whole – they frequently repeat the mantra that 'politicians are all the same, they are liars!' Imagine if these citizens were to take the same attitude to business leaders in charge of entities in which they have invested, especially against the background of the current persistent and deep financial crisis! In some ways there is more reason to be cynical of business leaders who have deliberately manipulated markets and created financial instruments of mass destruction of wealth for poor homeowners and workers, than the blanket condemnation of politicians.

There is an interesting contrast between the attitudes of many such wealthy people in how they behave as shareholders in the business world and their responses as citizens. Significant shareholders tend to take an active interest in the performance of the companies they invest in, and would not hesitate to show management the door at annual general meetings if the performance of the company was poor enough to warrant it. Ironically, the same people seem to ignore the reality that they are shareholders of their country's commonwealth. As shareholders, citizens have a major role to play in influencing the politics that ultimately shapes the environment in which business is conducted by their investee companies. Complaining around dinner tables might provide short-term comic relief but the cost of unaccountable politics is high for individuals and society as a whole.

The tragedy of silent free-riding business people is the high opportunity cost of their acquiescence to bad governance practices to protect their business interests. Take the case of undermining the policy intentions of Broad-Based Black Economic Empowerment Act, No. 53 of 2003. As indicated in the Introduction, experience far and wide across the globe points to the high risk of unintended consequences of empowerment programmes to address the legacy of discriminatory practices of previous regimes. Malaysia, which was our reference case, has had to blow the whistle on practices that enriched a few at the expense of many in the name of empowerment of indigenous people. The USA has also had to modify its Affirmative Action to minimise its negative impact on African-Americans, the very people it was meant to assist. Affirmative Action was found in some cases to reinforce the stereotypes that undermine African-American progress. The stereotype threat phenomenon – the fear of living out the negative perceptions that people hold of you or your social group – is real in a discriminatory social culture. Individuals facing this stereotype threat do better when they are simply allowed to perform without reference to their preferential regulatory entitlements.

The question facing our society in general, and business leaders in particular, is how we are going to extricate ourselves from the trap of unintended BEE consequences and focus on using all our considerable human and natural resources to grow our economy in an inclusive sustainable way. This is a question that citizens of our democracy must face and cannot simply defer to politicians. The voices of business leaders are missing in the debates that ought to inform the way forward beyond BEE which has been used by both politicians and captains of industry to enrich a few at the expense of many. Much looting of public resources has occurred in the name of empowerment at local government, provincial and national levels. It takes two to tango – business leaders are active participants in corruption, nepotism and abuse of state resources. The healing of past wounds cannot occur without honest conversations that also include what we have learnt over the last eighteen years and how we can use those lessons to forge a more sustainable development pathway.

One can only assume that many citizens believe that they are powerless to change the course of the political history in their own country. There can be no doubt that the electoral system which is based on closed party lists, except at the local level, undermines the value of each vote. Power in such an electoral system resides with party bosses and not voters. In exercising their vote, citizens are presented with no direct constituency representatives to choose from. The present electoral system was meant to be a bridging system which was to have been changed after five years, as explained in Chapter 4. It is now up to citizens, including you as the younger generation, to challenge the government to commit to putting the report of the Van Zyl Slabbert Commission up for public discussion and comment so we can deal with this unfinished agenda item on our journey to advance and strengthen our transition to democracy.

At the end of the day, the journey from subject to citizen can only be as successful as the level of active participation of all citizens permits. We need to challenge ourselves on how comfortable we feel that the values that drive our personal, professional and political selves are aligned to the demands of active citizenship. There is no place in a constitutional

Conversations with My Sons and Daughters

democracy for free-riding without paying the cost of living with the reality of an ineffectual state. The laudable National Development Plan released by our National Planning Commission on 11 November 2011 makes it abundantly clear that achieving the vision of a prosperous, diverse, multicultural and dynamic society is not achievable without an engaged citizenry. It is up to each of us to make the commitment to the journey towards the future we envisage for our beloved country.

Let us turn to the issue of leadership on this journey.

CHAPTER 9

LEADERSHIP FOR COMPLETING THE TRANSITION

We are again at a crossroads as a country. We managed the first transition to democracy by working together as civil society groups internally and later linked with the exiles in the liberation movement to achieve a glorious victory against apartheid. We are now challenged to complete the transition and make freedom a reality in the daily lives of ordinary citizens. Transitions succeed largely as a result of leadership that is focused on the goal of freedom and capable of inspiring citizens through leading by example.

In the language of the Dinokeng Scenarios, we can continue to 'walk apart' and/or 'walk behind' as we have tended to do, or we can begin the journey towards a different future and learn anew how to 'walk together'. Journeys often begin with conversations about where to, when, how, and with whom? Ours is no different. The chapters in this book thus far have addressed the first three questions. This concluding chapter focuses on the last question: with whom?

During the first few years of our transition we were blessed with able leadership that steered us towards a mass-based approach in the march to freedom. Our journey started in earnest with the 1950s ANC-led defiance campaigns, the 1960s PAC anti-pass laws campaigns, the 1970s Black Consciousness Movement student-led protests that gave way to labour and civic association mass mobilisations. The relentless bid for freedom ultimately overwhelmed what had up to then been seen as an impenetrable fortress of white domination. The leadership for this mass-based movement was provided by ordinary people: in street committees, SRCs, school committees, churches and other faith-based bodies, factory floors and in every situation in which people found themselves. They became, to paraphrase Mahatma Gandhi, the change they wanted to see in their own country.

Nelson Mandela, our founding father as first president, was the first to recognise the power of ordinary people and to leverage it to initiate settlement talks with his captors in jail. The liberation movement formations outside and inside the country also realised that the real liberators had to be the people themselves. The ANC in exile was forced by developments post-1976 into accepting the importance of complementing the internal mass-based challenges to the system of apartheid instead of undermining them. This internal mass-based movement became increasingly led by faith-based leaders such as Desmond Tutu, Archbishop Emeritus of the Anglican Church of Southern Africa,

Muslim scholar Farid Esack and the Reverend Allan Boesak of the Uniting Reformed Church. The focus internally was mass mobilisation against governance without representation of the majority, whereas the ANC outside mounted a successful propaganda programme that discredited the apartheid government. International pressure mounted and ultimately divestment and disinvestment in the apartheid economy undermined the foundations of white privilege. The stage was set for the successful negotiated settlement that ushered in the freedom we enjoy today.

President Mandela has at every available opportunity acknowledged the role played by ordinary citizens in attaining our freedom. He resisted attempts to rewrite history and to perpetuate the myth that his organisation, the ANC, was the sole contributor to the freedom so many sacrificed so much for. But Mandela also resisted the hero-worship that was showered on him. He insisted on affirming the role of others in the struggle for freedom, such as Walter Sisulu, Govan Mbeki and Ahmed Kathrada, rather than placing himself above his fellow citizens. He regarded himself as a servant leader who rose to the occasion history presented him with to lead his country to freedom. His famous words at his inauguration as president of the republic need to be repeated here:

> The time has come to heal the wounds. The moment to bridge the chasms that divide has come. The time to build is upon us ... We have triumphed in the effort to implant hope in the breasts of millions of our people. We enter into a covenant that we shall build the society in which all South Africans, both black and white, will be able to walk tall, without fear in their hearts, assured of their inalienable right to human dignity – a rainbow nation at peace with itself and the world.

As Mandela gazes into the sunset of his life in the familiar surroundings of Qunu, his Eastern Cape birthplace, we need to make sure we do not betray his legacy and that of so many who paid with their lives for our freedom. We need to heed his advice that our future can only be brighter if we commit to live our dream of a nation united in its diversity and driven by the recognition of the human dignity of all.

Your generation needs to reclaim the mantle of leadership that the young people of this country first wore in the late 1960s and 1970s when their parents were too afraid to confront the brutal apartheid regime. Today you not only have the advantage of an enabling constitutional democratic environment, but also the knowledge and professional skills unheard of in the 1970s, especially among young black people. You also have the advantage of having lived the dream of a rich diverse cultural milieu in the neighbourhoods, schools and workplaces you were privileged to grow up in. But the persistent and growing divide between the 'haves' and 'have-nots' is too glaring for you to ignore as you drive or walk the length and breadth of our cities, peri-urban and rural areas. Inequality and marginalisation of so many after nearly twenty years of freedom is the greatest risk you face as a generation. It also poses a grave risk for the future of your children.

I am appealing to your sense of social justice and self-interest to be part of the journey to consign to history the poverty and inequity in our country. Ours is a rich enough country to provide for the needs of all. We can put an end to our underperformance in the socio-economic domain relative to our peer countries by unleashing the energy trapped in our fellow citizens living on the margins of our society. The more than three million young people not in school, not in education, not in employment or training (NEETS) are a rich resource that is waiting for you, as young leaders, to help society tap into.

Imagine the impact of each one of you reaching out to at least one of these young people and helping them discover their potential talents and capabilities! Imagine the joy of watching them grow into more self-confident people with a sense of purpose with your mentorship and guidance! Imagine the day they graduate into independent artisans, artists, skilled workers in various fields or entrepreneurs in their own ventures! Imagine that first confident smile and the power of the wave as they fly away from being mentees to becoming mentors of the next wave of young people! Imagine! It is through such imagination that many of the ills of our society can be tackled systematically.

We need to stretch our imagination beyond the comfort zones of today's realities. We need to root out those approaches and practices that hold us back from openness to new and different ways of tackling our ongoing challenges. First and foremost, we need to change our mindsets and embrace the values of our democracy and learn to live them out in our daily encounters: at home, in our communities, in our workplaces and wider society. The 'I am because you are' – *Ubuntu* – should be the touchstone of our social relationships and we should distance ourselves from those who use *Ubuntu* as a slogan to market themselves in both the private and public sector without any intention of living its values.

We need to learn from other cultures as well about the importance of *Ubuntu*, especially in framing how we lead. Aung San Suu Kyi, the Burmese Nobel Prize winner, had this to say:

> The quintessential revolution is that of the spirit ... To live the full life one must have the courage to bear responsibility of the needs of others ... one *must want* to bear this responsibility.[90]

To what extent have we made the 'revolution of the spirit' our focus to guide our post-apartheid social relationships? Is it not true that instead of becoming the nation at peace that Mandela spoke of at his inauguration we have become much further apart? The process of healing has yet to begin and for that we need the humility of spirit to acknowledge the need for it and commit to work with others in our homes, community, at work and wider society to achieve it.

The second step allied to mindset change is the need for a new language to reflect the vision we are committed to. The journey from subject to citizen has to include discarding the expressions that promote the very passivity we seek to root out in out psycho-social relationships. Citizens are not passive recipients of whatever largesse comes from those in government or some other form of authority. The notion of 'service delivery' may have arisen from a desire by our first government to be seen to be 'delivering' on the promises of freedom. But no government in the world can have the capacity and resources to 'deliver services' on the scale needed to eradicate poverty and inequality to a passive citizenry. The language of 'delivery' reinforces the very subject identity that the Dinokeng 'walk together' approach is seeking to shift into a citizen identity characterised by the exercise of rights and responsibilities. Sustainable development is only possible through active engagement of citizens in all the phases of the process.

The process of becoming an active citizen involves confronting the fear that holds us back from taking the steps to live our values and hopes, making our voices heard on good and bad things in our society. Psychologist and author Nathaniel Branden has this to say to those of us who are afraid:

Innovators and creators are persons who can to a higher degree than average accept the condition of aloneness. They are more willing to follow their own vision, even if it takes them far from the mainland of human community. Unexplored places do not frighten them – or not, at any rate, as much as they frighten those around them. This is one of the secrets of their power. That which we call 'genius' has a great deal to do with courage and daring, a great deal to do with nerve.[91]

Our society needs you to be the geniuses that shed the mantle of fear in exchange for that of courage to lead us out of the morass of fear and false loyalties that undermine good governance and the building of bridges across the widening chasms in our society. You have the desire to live your and your country's dreams, but are you ready to use your knowledge, skills and youthful energy to be the leaders you have been waiting for?

The third step of our journey involves strengthening and deepening leadership among citizens. Heroic politics is limited in its ability to sustainably drive change precisely because of the narrow reach of leaders in a pyramidal system of power. One of the reasons for the resilience of the student-led Black Consciousness Movement (BCM) in the 1970s and that of the Mass Democratic Movement (MDM) in the 1980s was the practice of holding leadership development seminars and workshops that created safe spaces for activists to hone their leadership skills. Not everyone can be a leader in the traditional sense, but each one of us has leadership capabilities in niche areas that need to be identified and developed. Investing in people to develop into the best they can become is essential to unleashing the creative energy of latent talents in every individual that are sorely needed if our society is to grow itself into prosperity and greater equality.

The twenty-first century offers us even better opportunities to create real and virtual spaces to develop leadership especially among young people. The information technology revolution has been successfully used by both the private and public sector to drive development. The 2011 Arab Spring demonstrated the effectiveness of ICT to build civil society networks that eventually toppled dictators who had up until then looked invincible. We need to harness the power of ICT to discover our own ways of strengthening our democracy. We have the constitution, the institutions, the policies and examples of success to build on. But we also need to be brutally frank in naming our failures, harvesting the lessons of the last two decades and building a stronger leadership base to drive our socio-economic and political development.

What is striking about our society is how thin the layer of active leadership is, especially in the public sector. The private sector does a better job of leadership development than the public sector, but even so much more could be done in both sectors. Our academic institutions remain at risk as our top researchers, the majority of whom remain white and male, are mostly more than fifty years old. Fewer young people, black and white, are opting for academic careers. We need to put pressure on academic institutions to lead by example in creating innovative solutions in this area of human and intellectual capital development to enhance our country's competitiveness. The business sector has yet to let go of the 'old boy networks' that continue to hamper openness for recruitment, development and promotion of talents from young people across race and gender divides. We need to leverage the diversity of talents and capabilities which multiculturalism brings to the table.

The ineffectual and unaccountable state machinery identified as a binding constraint for our country's development reflects weak leadership within the public sector. Leadership weaknesses are visible not only in senior positions at the national, provincial and local levels across the country, but also at the middle and lower levels, and there is a crisis of leadership in our public service. This is not only a matter of concern within the governing party ranks, but across the spectrum of public service, with some notable exceptions. At the heart of our leadership woes is the impact of ignoring competence and integrity in appointments to positions in the public service. The appointment of people beyond their level of competence undermines capable people who have to work with such leaders and managers. The environment created by such appointments is one which is anti-intellectual, mediocre and lacking in integrity. It is inconceivable that such an environment can be an effective incubator of the leaders of tomorrow.

Cadre deployment is not in itself a problem. It is a worldwide practice of most political parties that come to power. The difference between successful nations and unsuccessful ones is whether or not deployees are matched to the requirements of the jobs and roles they are to fulfil. Our democracy has been characterised by a series of governments that did not take full advantage of the talents in our society. President Mandela's government had superior breadth and depth of leadership and management than subsequent ones.

What distinguished that first government from subsequent ones was the magnetism of Mandela as president and leader of government and the strong attraction and symbolism of being part of the historic transition. There was also a huge upsurge of idealism that saw many citizens, including senior private sector personalities such as Chris Liebenberg of Nedbank and Meyer Kahn of SA Breweries volunteer their services to contribute to the ushering in of the democratic order.

Mandela's style of leadership was enabling in that it was not threatened by being surrounded by people who knew much more than he did about the technical aspects of governance. He was a leader who believed in excellence as an essential element to ensuring equity in the provision of public services.

It is fair to say that subsequent leadership in government has paid less attention to excellence in their pursuit of equity. Competence as an essential criterion for appointment to public service jobs fell by the wayside. The level of incompetence as depicted by the 2011 Auditor General Reports is frightening and it is less a reflection of incompetent officials and more a symptom of leadership of the governing party that has thrown caution to the wind.

An example of lack of attention to competence and integrity was the 2009 appointment by President Zuma of Menzi Simelane, a former Director General of the Department of Justice under President Mbeki, to head the Directorate of the National Prosecution Authority (NPA). Menzi Simelane was found to be lacking in integrity in his evidence against then Director of the NPA, Vusi Pikoli, to the Ginwala Commission of Inquiry. The Ginwala Commission referred his case to the Public Service Commission to determine whether he was a fit and proper person to serve as a senior public servant. This referral was unfortunately not acted upon by President Mbeki. His successor, President Zuma, went further than simply ignoring the Commission's finding, but showed scant respect for due process by appointing Simelane to head the Directorate of the NPA. It came as no surprise to those committed to upholding the rule of law that the Appellate Division of the Supreme Court upheld the Democratic Alliance's case against President Zuma declaring Simelane's appointment to be improper.

The decline in the quality of leadership in our public service is also exemplified in parliament. The first parliament was a robust forum with a critical mass of highly skilled representatives, a significant proportion of whom had had international exposure. The Speaker of that first parliament, Frene Ginwala, was a woman of substance who drove the parliamentary agenda with passion and professionalism. Many MPs were people driven by the desire to serve and set the foundations of our democracy on a firm footing, the quality of debates was high and MPs were engaged in learning programmes to strengthen their ability to participate meaningfully in the affairs of governance. The National Council of Provinces, despite the ambiguities of its mandate, rose to the challenge under able leadership. That first parliament modelled servant leadership.

Today's parliament is a shadow of that first one. Notwithstanding the good leadership of the current Speaker, Max Sisulu, absenteeism, sleeping during sessions by overweight MPs, lack of a sense of urgency and professionalism characterise our parliamentary business. The TV channel that carries the daily proceedings of parliament is boring and often out of date and is not worth the trouble of watching it. The devaluing of parliament as a forum for holding government accountable is also reflected by how few ministers bother to go parliament to answer questions, and when they do the attitude of many of them seems to be disrespectful of MPs. Many parliamentary questions are answered in writing by officials but a significant number are simply ignored. In 2011, for instance, more than 360 questions raised by the DA had gone unanswered within the prescribed framework of ten working days, according to Ian Davidson of the DA,[92] although Deputy President Motlanthe later denied that questions were being ignored.[93]

This is yet another example of the distortion of accountability in a closed party list system where MPs are dependent on party bosses for their highly paid jobs. Many MPs see their job as defending ministers rather than holding them accountable to the citizens whom they are supposed to represent. The depth of weaknesses in the professionalism of the public service and their causes were dealt with in Chapter 3. The system is groaning under the lack of leadership from the top down. A dramatic and urgent change is needed if we are to meet even the most basic national goals we have set for ourselves.

Your leadership is urgently needed. You are in a good position to take up your responsibilities as leaders in the twenty-first century by learning from the experiences of your peers in our interconnected world. The Arab Spring of 2011 demonstrated that where there is a will there is a way to change even the most inflexible system. Young people in North Africa and the Middle East have taken on unaccountable leaders and won. The invincibility of tyrants melted in the face of determined citizens who were prepared to pay the ultimate price for their freedom. You are in a fortunate position of not needing to face the dangers they faced. Ours is a constitutional democracy in which you are the sovereigns – you are the ultimate custodians of this democracy. Your rights and responsibilities are guaranteed by the national constitution. Your duty is to be engaged in your stewardship role.

The Dinokeng Scenarios referred to in Chapter 7 painted three scenarios: *walk apart*, *walk behind* and *walk together*. There is a fourth scenario. Engaged citizens have a right and a responsibility to *walk ahead* in situations in which state organs, such as the executive and the legislature, are dragging their feet on matters of national public interest. Arab Spring leaders have already blazed the trail by walking ahead of their governments and parents who were too afraid to challenge tyranny. You have the example of the 1976 youth leaders who took on the apartheid system and many paid the ultimate price for your freedom. The time for your generation to lead is now. Demography is on your side – the 16 to 40 year age group makes up the largest proportion of the population.

You have the power to change by opening yourself to what Aung San Suu Kyi refers to as 'the quintessential revolution of the spirit'. We have accomplished a revolution in constitutional, policy and general participatory governance terms. What is missing is mindset change, or the revolution of the spirit, which starts with you at the personal, professional and political levels. Transformative leadership demands change from within which paves the way for modelling the change you want to see. Your generation has to meet the challenge of your destiny – completing the work started on the covenant Nelson Mandela committed to: '… we shall build the society in which all South Africans, both black and white, will be able to walk tall, without fear in their hearts, assured of their inalienable right to human dignity – a rainbow nation at peace with itself and the world.'

Are you ready to meet your destiny?

ENDNOTES

1   South African Institute of Race Relations (SAIRR) Annual Survey, 2009/2010, p260

2   Fiona Forde (2011), *An Inconvenient Youth: Julius Malema*, Picador Africa, p169

3   Ibid

4   Information freely available on Google website Chancellor House Holdings

5   Frantz Fanon (1968), *The Wretched of the Earth*, New York: Grove Press, p206

6   Nigel C Gibson (2011), *Fanonian Practices in South Africa*, UKZN Press and Palgrave Macmillan, p110

7   Borrowing from Nigel Gibson's words in *Fanonian Practices in South Africa*, p42

8   Stephen Biko (1978), *I Write what I Like*, London: Bowerdean Press

9   HSRC 2006 as cited in Lucy Holborn & Gail Eddy (2011), *First Steps to Healing the South African Family*, SAIRR, p2

10   Child Gauge 2010/2011, University of Cape Town, p80

11   Holborn & Eddy, op cit

12   Mid-Year population estimates (StatsSA) estimate that the 15-35 year age group population stands at 36.99%. Source: http://www.statssa.gov.za/publications/P0302/P03022011.pdf

13   SAIRR 2009/2010 Survey, p186

14   Ibid, p203

15   NPC Diagnostic Review, 2011, p11

16   I Serageldin, 'The Challenge of Science in Building Democracy', Panel Discussion at Nelson Mandela Foundation, 22 July 2011

17   See the work of Elinor Ostrom, 2009 Nobel Prize Winner for Economics

18   Richard Wilkinson & Kate Pickett (2010), *The Spirit Level: Why equality is better for everyone*, London: Penguin, p205

19   Annexures: Summary of data of all municipalities. Local Government Budget and Expenditure Review, p237

20   Theodore Sturgeon, 'The Wages of Synergy' (short story), 1953

21   Carl Jung (1995), *Memories, Dreams and Reflections*, HarperCollins, p362

22   Andrew Feinstein (2007), *After The Party: A personal and political journey inside the ANC*, Cape Town and Johannesburg: Jonathan Ball

23   Frantz Fanon (1967), *Black Skin, White Masks* as quoted in Nigel Gibson, op cit, p44

24   TNS Research Surveys (Pty) Ltd and UCT Unilever Institute research findings

25   Caution needs to be exercised in evaluating this buying power as we now know that much of it was inflated by credit expansion that has become more evident and is driving the global financial crisis

26   *Saturday Star*, 30 October 2011

27   South Africa Economic Update, July 2011

28   Raymond Aron in F W Wilson & M Ramphele (1989), *Uprooting Poverty: The South African Challenge*, Cape Town: David Philip

29   Richard Wilkinson & Kate Pickett, op cit, p4

30   Alan Gelb, Ali A G Ali, Tesfaye Dinka, Ibrahim Elbadawi, Charles Soludo & Gene Tidrick (2000), 'Can Africa Claim the 21st Century?' World Bank Report

31   Moeletsi Mbeki (2009), *Architects of Poverty: Why African Capitalism Needs Changing*, Picador Africa – Pan Macmillan

32   Prince Mashele (2011), *The Death of Our Society*, CPR Press, p1

33   Ibid

34   Ben Turok (ed.) (2011), *Understanding the ANC Today* series, Johannesburg: Jacana Media

35   Attahiru Jega (ed) (2000), *Identity Transformation and Identity Politics under Structural Adjustment in Nigeria*, Afrikainstitutet and Centre for Research and Documentation, p15

36   R Hall (2004), 'A political economy of land reform in South Africa', *Review of African Political Economy*, No.100; and SAIRR, 2010, citing the Department of Agriculture and Land Affairs, The Land and Agrarian Reform Project: The Concept Document, pp7–35, February 2008; The Presidency, *Development Indicators 2009*, 2009, p34; National Assembly Internal Question Paper No 1–2010, Question 167, 11 February 2010

37   As cited in SAIRR Source: The Presidency, Development Indicators 2009, p34, 2009.

38   IOL News on Line on Google

39   Africa's leading statistical assessment of governance, created by the Mo Ibrahim

Foundation

40   See Janet Smith & Beauregard Tromp (2002), *Hani: A Life Too Short*, Cape Town and Johannesburg: Jonathan Ball; *Slovo: The Unfinished Autobiography*, 2002, Ocean Press

41   Mark Gevisser (2007), *Thabo Mbeki: The Dream Deferred*, Johannesburg and Cape Town: Jonathan Ball

42   Ibid, p739

43   Thabo Mbeki, 'He Wakened to His Responsibilities', Inaugural Z K Matthews Memorial Lecture, University of Fort Hare, 12 October 2001

44   Mark Gevisser, op cit, p284

45   J K Birnbaum, C J L Murray & R Lozano (2011), 'Exposing misclassified HIV/ AIDS deaths in South Africa, *Bulletin of the World Health Organisation*, 89: 278-285

46   DBSA Development Report for 2011

47   The South African Screen Federation released the Young Communist League press statement on the planned mass action to the SABC. 'The current SABC board was illegitimately appointed through improper and underhand intervention in the parliamentary process to achieve narrow political objectives. The board therefore lacks legitimacy and no amount of manoeuvring can give it the legitimacy required for the leadership of a national asset. The current SABC board has plunged the SABC into a situation in which its very survival is threatened, lurching from one crisis to the next since its appointment two years ago.' http://www.ngopulse.org/sites/default/files/SOS_ Campaign_Press_statement_on_the_mass_action_to_the_SABC.pdf

48   Report on http://www.sahrc.org website

49   Van Zyl Slabbert Commission on Electoral Reform on http://www. nelsonmandela.org website

50   http://www.miami.com/mld/miamiherald/business/special_packages/ business_monday/13527922.htm?source=rss&channel=miamiherald_ business_monday

51   DBSA Health Hospital Assessment, 2011

52   AG Reports – see also new AG website plus Report by Department of Local and Co-operative Government on facts and figures

53   Source: Union Africa Action Plan for boosting intra-African trade, African

Union

54 Source: Overlapping Membership in COMESA, EAC, SACU AND SADC. Trade Policy Options for the Region and for EPA negotiations

55 Source: Ainalem Tebeje, 'Brain drain and capacity building in Africa', Association for Higher Education and Development (AHEAD), International Development Research Center (IDRC), Ottawa http://www.idrc.ca/EN/ Resources/Publications/Pages/ArticleDetails.aspx?PublicationID=704

56 http://www.vocfm.co.za/index.php?option=com_ k2&view=item&id=3369:new-dose-of-xenophobia&ltemid=131

57 J F Kennedy, Special message to the Congress on Education, 20/02/1961, as quoted by Richard Wilkinson and Kate Pickett, op cit, p103

58 SACMEQ III

59 The number of teachers in South Africa was 232 160 in 2009, according to a World Bank report published in 2010. The number of primary education teachers in South Africa was reported as 238 900 in 2008, according to the World Bank. Primary education teachers includes full-time and part-time teachers. Source: http://www.tradingeconomics.com/south-africa/primary-education-teachers-wb-data.html

60 HSRC collaborative study with Stanford University, still work in progress

61 Model C School category was introduced in the dying days of apartheid as a compromise solution to the reality of some of these schools defying the government by admitting black children

62 *City Press*, 27 February 2011

63 UNICEF Basic Indicator Table (stats based on Inter-agency Group for Child Mortality Estimation, UNICEF, World Health Organisation, United Nations Population Division and the World Bank. Published in 2012

64 Source: 'Maternal and Infant Mortality Expert Hopeful for SA', *South African Medical Journal*, Vol 100, No 3, March 2010

65 Source: Sian Floyd et al, UNICEF project: HIV and orphanhood: final report on phase 3, September 2005. This report concerns the third phase of a project using empirical evidence from longitudinal, community-based studies in Africa to assess the overall impact of the HIV epidemic on child welfare

66 Source: Teenage Pregnancy in South Africa with a special focus on school-going learners. UNICEF and South African Government Document, 2009

67 Source: UNICEF Basic Indicators

68 Pre-2009 elections that put Jacob Zuma in the presidency, the DBSA led a process of reviewing and recommending 10 urgent actions to reform the underperforming education system

69 Malcolm Gladwell (2008), *Outliers: The Story of Success*, New York: Little, Brown & Co, p249

70 Malcolm Gladwell, op cit, from Chapter 8: 'Rice Paddies and Math Tests'. This idea builds on the work of Stanislas Dehaene (*The Number Sense: How the Mind Creates Mathematics*, revised and updated edition, New York: Oxford University Press, 2011). He argues that because Chinese names for numbers are so short, Chinese people can remember up to nine or ten digits at a time – English-speaking people can only remember seven

71 Dinokeng is a Sesotho word for 'a place of rivers or a place where rivers converge'. It is a farming district situated north of Pretoria in Gauteng Province. We liked the symbolism of the metaphor – it captured the convergence of the minds of Team members to focus on securing a better future for our country

72 Dinokeng Scenarios Team members: Miriam Altman, Frans Baleni, Ann Bernstein, Nkosinathi Biko, Cheryl Carolus, Angela Coetzee, Ryan Coetzee, Paul Hanratty, Bob Head, Haniff Hoosen, Moemedi Kepadisa, Reuel Khoza, Kallie Kriel, Antje Krog, Graça Machel, Mary Malete, Vincent Maphai, Rick Menell, Daniel Mminele, Namhla Mniki, Aaron Motsoaledi, Jay Naidoo, Yogan Naidoo, Njongonkulu Ndungane, Maite Nkoana-Mashabane, Thandi Nontenja, Thami ka Plaatjie, Mamphela Ramphele, Sonja Sebotsa, Raenette Taljaard, Mathatha Tsedu, Sim Tshabalala, Musi Zondi

73 I was privileged to Chair the Conveners of Dinokeng Scenarios who included: Njongonkulu Ndungane, Vincent Maphai, Rick Mennell, Reuel Khoza and Graça Machel

74 Njabulo Ndebele, Meditating on Corruption, *City Press* article, 22 January 2012

75 Source: Portfolio Committee on Finance, Mineral and Petroleum Resource Royalty Bill Response Document, 13 May 2008

76 Richard Wilkinson & Kate Pickett, op cit , p210

77 Carl Jung (1995), *Memories, Dreams and Reflections*, HarperCollins, p357

78 http://aboutsuffering.blogspot.com/2006/10/physicalsocial-pain-overlap-theory.html

79   As quoted in Richard Wilkinson & Kate Pickett, op cit

80   Martha Cabrera, www.communitas.co.za

81   Quoted by Emily Nagisa Keehn & Dean Peacock, *Mail & Guardian*, June 3-9 2011

82   Ibid

83   *Mail & Guardian* June 3-9 2011, 'The Strong Arm of the Force'

84   Mahmood Mamdani (1996), *Citizen and Subject: Contemporary Africa and the Legacy of Late Colonialism*, Princeton University Press

85   Martha Cabrera transcribed talk with Envio

86   http//www.aadnc-aandc.gc.ca/aiarch/mr/nr/m-a2009/bk000000351-eng.asp

87   A slum in East London in the Eastern Cape

88   Participants included Atlantic Philanthropies (the Sponsor), DFID, EU, Gold Fields and Eskom representatives

89   *Fanonian Practices* referred to in Chapter 3

90   Peter Popham (2011), *The Lady and the Peacock: The Life of Aung San Suu Kyi*, Random House, p301

91   Nathaniel Branden, Quote from Google

92   Source: Parliament's unanswered questions. Lynley Donnelly (26 August 2011) http://mg.co.za/article/2011-08-26-parliaments-unanswered-questions

93   Source: http://www.thepresidency.gov.za/pebble.asp?relid=5823&t=79